FamilyCircle®

easy
accessories

50 chic projects to knit and crochet

Family Circle®

easy
accessories

50 chic projects to knit and crochet

sixth&spring books
New York

Sixth&Spring Books
233 Spring Street
New York, NY 10013

Editorial Director
Trisha Malcolm

Art Director
Chi Ling Moy

Book Division Manager
Erica Smith

Graphic Designer
Sheena Thomas

Yarn Editor
Veronica Manno

Technical Editors
Carla Scott, Karen Greenwald, Pat Harste

Production Manager
David Joinnides

President and Publisher, Sixth&Spring Books
Art Joinnides

Family Circle Magazine

Editor-in-Chief
Susan Kelliher Ungaro

Consulting Editor
Barbara Winkler

Creative Director
Diane Lamphron

Copyright© 2005 by Sixth&Spring Books
All rights reserved including the right of reproduction in whole or
in part in any form.

Library of Congress Catalog-in-Publication Data
Library of Congress Control Number: 2005922328
ISBN 1-931543-85-2
ISBN-13 978-1-931543-85-9

Manufactured in China

Table of Contents

wrap it up

These styles prove you don't
need sleeves to stay warm and
look wonderful.

8

sixth sense

Just because winter is setting in, don't set aside your passion for color! This poncho, made of six color squares, will keep you feeling rosy all season. Designed by Jean Guirguis, "Sixth Sense" first appeared in the Winter '04/'05 issue of *Family Circle Easy Knitting*.

MATERIALS

Museum by Artful Yarns/JCA, Inc., 3½oz/100g balls, each approx 76yd/70m (wool)

- 1 ball each in #7 green, #9 multi,
  #4 red, #5 blue, #2 brown and #3 purple
- One pair size 13 (9mm) needles OR SIZE TO OBTAIN GAUGE
- 2yd/1.85m Tejas leather lace in brown

FINISHED MEASUREMENTS

Approx 31" x 25"/78.5 x 63.5cm

GAUGE

9 sts and 14 rows to 4"/10cm over St st using size 13 (9mm) needles.
TAKE TIME TO CHECK YOUR GAUGE.

PONCHO SQUARES (MAKE 6)

Working 1 square in each color, cast on 27 sts. Work in St st for 12"/30.5cm. Bind off.

FINISHING

Placing colors as desired, join squares together (see photo), using St st as RS for top 2 squares of poncho and reverse St st as RS for lower square of poncho.

For neckline, weave leather lace from top point of lower square to distance desired for neckline.

FRINGE

Cut 9 10"/25.5cm strands of coordinating yarn and attach to each square.

confetti confab

Worked in a cheerful color palette, this openwork scarf/wrap hybrid is a breeze to make in garter stitch. Designed by Suzan Lee, it can be tied, twisted, knitted, or draped and lends ample versatility and spice to any outfit. "Confetti Confab" first appeared in the Spring/Summer '05 issue of *Family Circle Easy Knitting*.

MATERIALS

Trellis by Lion Brand Yarn, 1¾oz/50g balls, each approx 115yd/105m (nylon)

   6 balls in #306 pastel garden

   Size 15 (10mm) circular needle, 24"/60cm long, OR SIZE TO OBTAIN GAUGE

FINISHED MEASUREMENTS

   Approx 14" x 150"/35.5 x 381cm

GAUGE

   8 sts and 10 rows over 4"/10cm in yo pat st [2 repeats of (4 rows garter st, 1 yo row)] using size 15 (10mm) needles. TAKE TIME TO CHECK YOUR GAUGE.

Note

   Use 1 strand A and B held together throughout.

SCARF

Cast on 300 sts loosely. Work in garter st for 3 rows.

Yo row *Insert needle knitwise, yo 3 times and complete knit st; rep from * for each st across. Work in garter st for 4 rows, dropping extra yo lps on row following yo row.

Rep last 5 rows 5 times more; work yo row, 3 rows garter st. Bind off loosely.

pleasantly pink

Be ready for compliments when you slip on in this old-fashioned shawl. Designer Pat Harste achieves the look with a triple-cross-stitch pattern and a frilly border that gives a girlish sense of movement while also maintaining lush texture. "Pleasantly Pink" first appeared in the Spring/Summer '03 issue of *Family Circle Easy Knitting*.

MATERIALS

Helen's Lace by Lorna's Laces Yarns, 4oz/125g hanks, each approx 1250yd/1143m (silk/wool)

   2 hanks in #10 peach

   Size E/4 (3.5mm) crochet hook OR SIZE TO OBTAIN GAUGE

FINISHED MEASUREMENTS

66"/167.5cm wide by 38"/96.5cm long

GAUGE

   30 sts and 13 rows to 4"/10cm over pat st using size E/4 (3.5mm) crochet hook.

   TAKE TIME TO CHECK YOUR GAUGE.

STITCH GLOSSARY

Triple Cross (TC)

Sk next 2 sts. Dc in 3rd st, dc in 2nd skipped st, dc in first skipped st.

SHAWL

Beg at bottom point, ch 8.

Row 1 (WS) Work 2 dc in 4th ch from hook, dc in next 3 ch, work 2 dc in last ch—7 sts. Ch 3, turn. **Row 2** Work 3 dc in first st, dc in next st, TC over next 3 sts, dc in next st, work 3 dc in last st—11 sts. Ch 3, turn. **Row 3** Work 3 dc in first st, *TC over next 3 sts; rep from *, end work 3 dc in last st—15 sts. Ch 3, turn. **Row 4** Work 3 dc in first st, dc in next 2 sts, *TC over next 3 sts; rep from *, end dc in next 2 sts, work 3 dc in last st—19 sts. Ch 3, turn. **Row 5** Work 3 dc in first st, dc in next st, *TC over next 3 sts; rep from *, end dc in next st, work 3 dc in last st—23 sts. Ch 3, turn. **Row 6** Work 3 dc in first st, *TC over next 3 sts; rep from *, end work 3 dc in last st—sts. Ch 3, turn. Rep rows 4-6 35 times more—111 rows completed (piece should measure approx 35"/89cm from beg).

Edging

Ch 1, turn. **Rnd 1 (RS)** Sc in each dc across last row made, then making sure that work lies flat, sc evenly across each side edge. Join rnd with a sl st in ch-1. Ch 5, turn. Work back and forth across side edges only.

Ruffle

Row 1 (WS) Skip first st, sc in next st, *ch 5, skip next st, sc in next st; rep from * to end. Ch 5, turn. **Rows 2-9** *Sc in next ch-5 lp, ch 5; rep from *, end sc in last st. Ch 5, turn. After row 9 is completed, ch 1, turn. **Row 10 (RS)** Work 5 sc in each ch-5 lp across. Fasten off.

FINISHING

Block piece to measurements.

Beaded trim

With RS facing, join yarn with a sl st in last edging skipped st on row 1 of ruffle. Working from left to right and in skipped sts of row 1 of ruffle, work as foll: hdc in same st, ch 1, *hdc in next skipped st, ch 1; rep from * across each side edge, end hdc in last skipped st. Fasten off.

cape fearless

This warm and whimsical capelet shows off your style and it's a cinch to create in basic garter stitch. The faux fur collar adds a touch of texture and plenty of glamour! Designed by Stephanie Klose, "Cape Fearless" appeared in the Winter '04/'05 issue of *Family Circle Easy Knitting*.

MATERIALS

Homespun by Lion Brand Yarns, 6oz/170g balls, each approx 185yd/167m (acrylic/polyester)

  2 balls in #336 blue (A)

  Fun Fur by Lion Brand Yarns, 1¾oz/50g balls, each approx 64yd/58m (polyester)

  2 balls each in #106 bright blue (B) and #170 peacock (C)

  One pair size 13 (9mm) needles OR SIZE TO OBTAIN GAUGE

  Size N-P/15 (10mm) crochet hook

FINISHED MEASUREMENTS

  Width at lower edge 46"/117cm

  Length 15"/38cm

GAUGE

  11 sts and 17 rows to 4"/10cm over St st using smaller needles and Homespun.

  TAKE TIME TO CHECK YOUR GAUGE.

CAPELET

With A, cast on 126 sts. Work in garter st for 5 rows, slipping first st of every row.

Next row (WS) Sl 1, k3, p to last 4 sts, k4. Cont as established, working first and last 4 sts in garter st, center sts in St st and slipping 1st st at beg of every row until piece measures 15"/38cm from beg. Cut A. Join 1 strand each B and C held tog and work in garter st for 8"/20.5cm. Bind off loosely.

FINISHING

Fold Fun Fur collar to RS. With crochet hook and A, working through both thicknesses, work a row of sc tightly along neck edge to pull in piece to measure approx 36"/91.5cm around.

TIES (MAKE 2)

With smaller needles and A, cast on 5 sts. Sl 1, k to end. Work in garter st, slipping first st every row, until piece measures 12"/30.5cm from beg. Bind off. Sew 1 tie to each front edge of capelet where Homepsun and Fun Fur sections meet.

snow white

Mari Lynn Patrick's crocheted stole is big on texture thanks to a lively shell-stitch pattern surrounded by a broad pineapple-stitch border. Add fringe and you've got a look that's fun without being flashy. "Snow White" first appeared in the Winter '03/'04 issue of *Family Circle Easy Knitting.*

MATERIALS

Pleasure by Berroco, Inc., 1³⁄₄oz/50g balls, each approx 130yd/120m (angora/wool/nylon)

    10 balls in #8601 white

    Size K/10½ (6.5mm) crochet hook OR SIZE TO OBTAIN GAUGE

FINISHED MEASUREMENTS

    20"/51cm wide x 74"/188cm long excluding fringe

GAUGE

    One shell pat to 2³⁄₄"/7cm wide and 4 rows of pat to 2½"/6.5cm.

    TAKE TIME TO CHECK YOUR GAUGE.

Size

    Shawl in one size

STITCH GLOSSARY

Shell Stitch

*Working into one designated st, [yo, insert hook into st, yo, pull lp through st, yo, pull through 2 lps] 3 times in same st, yo hook, pull through 4 lps on hook *, ch 3; rep between *'s once, ch 3, rep between *'s once more for shell st.

Pineapple Stitch

Working into designated st, *[yo, insert hook into st, pull up a lp] 3 times in same st, yo and pull through all 6 lps on hook, yo, pull through last 2 lps, ch 1*; rep between *'s for pineapple st.

SHAWL

Ch 44.

Row 1 (RS) Work 1 shell st in 4th ch from hook, *ch 2, skip 3 ch, 1 sc in next ch, ch 3, skip 3 ch, 1 sc in next ch, ch 2, skip 3 ch, 1 shell st in next ch; rep from *, end ch 2, skip 3 ch, 1 sc in last ch. Turn. There are 4 shell stitches with 3 clusters in each shell.

Row 2 Ch 5, *work (1 dc, ch 1 and 1 dc) in ch-3 sp between first 2 clusters of shell, work (1 dc, ch 1, and 1 dc) between the 2nd and 3rd clusters of same shell**, then work (1 dc, ch 3 and 1 dc) in the 2nd ch of the ch-3 sp between the 2 sc; rep from *, ending last rep at **, then ch 2, 1 dc in top of ch-3. Turn.

Row 3 Ch 4, *1 sc in ch-1 sp between the 2 dc, ch 3, 1 sc in next ch-1 sp between the 2 dc, ch 2, 1 shell st in the next ch-3 loop, ch 2; rep from *, end 1 sc in ch 1-sp, ch 3, 1 sc in ch-1 sp ch 2, 1 dc in the 3rd ch of t-ch. Turn.

Row 4 Ch 3, *work (1 dc, ch 3 and 1 dc) in 2nd ch of the ch-3 sp between the 2 sc, work (1 dc, ch 1 and 1 dc) between the first 2 clusters of shell, work (1 dc, ch 1 and 1 dc) between the next 2 clusters of shell; rep from *, end ch 2, dc in 3rd ch of t-ch. Turn.

Row 5 Ch 3, working as for row 1, *work 1 shell in ch-3 sp, ch 2, 1 sc in next ch-1 sp, ch 3, 1 sc in next ch-1 sp, ch 2; rep from *, end omit last ch 2, 1 dc in dc. Turn. Rep rows 2-5 for pat until piece measures approx 68"/172.5cm, end with pat row 4. Turn.

Edging

Rnd 1 (RS) Ch 1, *work 32 sc along first short edge working 2 sc in last st, work 2 sc in first st along (long) side edge, work 173 sc along side edge, 2 sc in last sc, 2 sc in first sc of short edge; rep from * once. Join with sl st.

Rnd 2 Ch 1, working in sc, work 1 sc in each sc with 2 st in last sc of each edge and 2 sc in first sc of next corner edge. Join with sl st.

Rnd 3 Ch 3, work 1 pineapple st in first sc, *skip 1 sc, work 1 pineapple st in next sc; rep from * to corner, 1 pineapple st in corner st, ch 3, 1 pineapple st in next st; rep from * around, end join with sl st to top of ch-3.

Rnd 4 Ch 1, work 1 sc in each pineapple st and 1 sc in each ch-1 sp with 4 sc in each ch-3 corner around.

Rnd 5 Ch 1, work 1 sc in each sc and ch 2 in each corner around.

Rnd 6 Ch 2, *[yo, insert hook into st, yo and pull up a lp, yo and pull through 2 lps] 3 times in same st, yo and pull through 4 lps**, ch 3; rep between * and ** once in same st (for flower st) skip 3 sts; rep from * to 2 sts before corner ch-2 sp, skip 2 sts, work flower st in corner, then skip 2 sts and rep from * around.

Rnd 7 Ch 1, working in sc, work 2 sc in each ch-3 sp, 1 sc in top of one flower petal and 1 sc between each flower (4 sc for every flower) and 4 sc in each corner ch-3 sp around.

Rnd 8 Rep rnd 2.

Rnd 9 Rep rnd 3.

Rnd 10 Rep rnd 4.

Rnd Rep rnd 5. Fasten off.

FINISHING

Lay shawl flat and block to measurements.

Fringe

Cut 4 lengths of 13"/33cm lengths for each fringe. Pull through 14 fringes along each end covering the 2 sc rows and skipping 2 pineapple sts across.

lavender lovely

Designed by Mickey Landau, this romantic capelet will inspire fantasies of high tea in an English garden. "Lavender Lovely" first appeared in the Spring/Summer '05 issue of *Family Circle Easy Knitting.*

MATERIALS

Dream by Moda Dea/Coats & Clark, 1¾oz/50g balls, each approx 93yd/85m (nylon/acrylic)

- 5 balls #3705 blush
- One pair size 10 (6mm) needles OR SIZE TO OBTAIN GAUGE
- Size 10 (6mm) circular needle, 24"/60cm long
- Size G/6 (4mm) crochet hook

FINISHED MEASUREMENTS

- Around bottom of cape approx 54"/137cm
- Length from shoulder to bottom edge approx 14"/35.5cm

GAUGE

4 sts and 20 rows over St st using size 10 (6mm) needles.
TAKE TIME TO CHECK YOUR GAUGE.

Note

Capelet is worked in one piece from bottom edge to shoulder.

CAPELET

With circular needle, cast on 186 sts. Work in St st for 5"/12.5cm, end with a RS row.

Next row (WS) P13, [pm, p23] 3 times, pm, p22, [pm, p23] 3 times, pm, p13.

COLLAR AND SHOULDER SHAPING

Row 1 (RS) K 1, inc 1 purlwise for beg of collar shaping, *k to 2 sts before marker, ssk, sl marker, k2tog; rep from * 7 times more, k to 2 sts before end of row, inc 1 purlwise for beg of opposite collar shaping, k1—16 dec and 2 inc made—172 sts.

Row 2 K3, p to last 3 sts, k3.

Row 3 K1, p2, k to last 3 sts, p2, k1.

Row 4 Rep row 2.

Row 5 K1, inc 1 purlwise, p1, k to last 3 sts, p1, inc 1 purlwise, k1—174 sts.

Row 6 K4, p to last 4 sts, k4.

Row 7 (dec row) K1, p3, *k to 2 sts before first marker, ssk, sl marker, k2tog; rep from * 7 times more, k to 4 sts before end of row, p3, k1—16 sts dec—158 sts.

Rep dec row every 6th row 5 times more, AT SAME TIME, inc 1 st (purlwise on RS rows, knitwise on WS rows) after first st and before last st on every 4th row 5 times more, every 3rd row 3 times and every other row 6 times, end with a WS row—106 sts.

Final dec row (RS) K1, p17, [k to 2 sts before next marker, ssk, sl marker] 4 times, [k to next marker, sl marker, k2tog] 4 times, p17, k1—98 sts (1 edge st, 17 collar sts, 62 back neck sts, 17 collar sts, 1 edge st).

Next row Change to straight needles and work across edge st and collar sts as established, join new ball of yarn, bind off center 62 sts, work across collar sts and edge st.

Work each side separately on straight needles in pat as established until collar pieces are long enough to meet at center back neck, slightly stretched. Bind off.

FINISHING

Sew collar seam; sew collar to back neck of capelet.

EDGING

With crochet hook and knit side of capelet facing, join yarn with sl st at beg of collar shaping on left front; working toward bottom of capelet, work *(sc, ch 8, sc) in next st or row, ch 8; rep from * along left front, bottom edge and right front to beg of collar. Fasten off. With knit side of collar facing, join yarn with sl st at beg of collar shaping on left front and work same edging around outside edge of collar. Fasten off.

TIES (MAKE 2)

With crochet hook and 2 strands of yarn held tog, ch 66. Cut 1 strand, leaving a 3"/7.5cm end.

FLOWER

Cont with single strand, work sc into last 2-strand ch made, (ch 8, sc) 5 times in same ch, (ch 8, sc) twice in next 2-strand ch st, ch 8, (sc, ch 8, sc) in opposite side of same 2-strand ch as first sc of flower, ch 8, join with sl st to first sc. Fasten off. Sew beg end of 2-strand chain to backside of flower to form a lp. Weave in yarn end.

JOIN TIE TO CAPELET

Insert hook from WS to RS of cape just below beg of collar shaping, pick up lp end of tie and pull to WS, insert flower end through lp and pull flower end to tighten. Join rem tie in same way to opposite side of collar.

red all over

This easy hooded style can be thrown on whether you're hailing a cab or heading to the park. A piece as sophisticated as it is rustic, it's merely two rectangles finished with crab stitching. An even bigger plus? It can be created by hand or machine. Designed by Betsy Westman, "Red All Over" first appeared in the Fall '02 issue of *Family Circle Easy Knitting*.

MATERIALS

Tussock 14 ply by Naturally/SR Kertzer, 3½oz/100g balls, each approx 124yd/ 115m (wool)

- 14 balls in #571 red (MC)
- 1 ball in #569 navy (CC)
- One pair size 9 (5.5 mm) needles OR SIZE TO OBTAIN GAUGE
- Size J/10 (6mm) crochet hook
- 7"/18cm zipper

FINISHED MEASUREMENTS

- Width 44"/112cm
- Length 28"/71cm

GAUGE

Handknit

15 sts and 20 rows to 4"/10cm over St st using size 9 (5.5 mm) needles.

Machine knit

14 sts and 20 rows to 4"/10cm using a #4 keyplate in st st.
TAKE TIME TO CHECK YOUR GAUGE.

Notes

1) Panels in both hand knit and machine knit versions are worked from back to front.

2) Hood is handknit in both versions.

Size

One size shown

HAND KNIT PONCHO

Left Side Panel

With MC, cast on 83 sts. Work in St st until piece measures 27½"/70cm from beg.

Neck shaping

Next row (RS) Bind off 16 sts, work to end. Work 1 row even. Inc 1 st at neck edge on next row, then every other row twice more, then every row 4 times. **Next row (RS)** Cast on 2 sts, work to end. Work 1 row even. Next row (RS) Cast on 7 sts, work to end—83 sts. Work even until piece measures 56"/142cm from beg. Bind off.

Right Side Panel

Work to correspond to left side panel, reversing neck shaping.

FINISHING

Block pieces to measurements. Sew center back seam. Sew center front seam beg 4"/10cm from neck shaping and working down center front. With crochet hook and CC, work 1 row sc around the outside of garment. Do not turn. Work 1 row backwards sc (from left to right). Fasten off.

HOOD

With MC and RS facing, pick up and k7 sts across right front neck, 15 sts up right side, 14 sts across right back neck, pm at center back hood, pick up and k14 sts across left back neck, 15 sts down left side, 7 sts across left front neck—72 sts. Work in St st for 11"/28cm. Next (dec) row (RS) Knit to within 2 sts of marker, ssk, slip marker, k2tog, knit to end. Rep dec row every other row twice more, then every row 4 times—58

sts. Place 29 sts on separate needle and with right sides facing, work 3 needle bind-off. With crochet hook and CC, work 1 row sc around hood edge and down center front opening. Do not turn. Work 1 row backwards sc (from left to right). Fasten off.

Sew zipper in center front opening.

MACHINE KNIT PONCHO

Left Side Panel

Bring forward 74 needles to HP. With MC, cast on using the closed edge method. Knit 140 rows ending COR. Bind off 15 sts for back neck at neck edge. Work 1 row. Inc 1 st neck edge every other row 3 times, then every row 3 times. In the next row cast on 2 sts at neck edge; work 1 row; cast on 7 sts at neck edge in the next row to 74 sts. Work without shaping until 284 rows from beg. Bind off loosely using the chain st method. Insert needles in beg edge and bind off.

Right Side Panel

Work to correspond to left side panel, reversing shaping.

FINISHING AND HOOD

Work same as hand knit version.

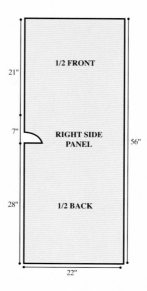

bonny blue

Make a bold statement in this playful ribbon-trim poncho by Stephanie Klose. An oversized crochet hook creates open stitches for an airy effect. "Bonny Blue" first appeared in the Winter '04/'05 issue of *Family Circle Easy Knitting*.

MATERIALS

Colorwaves by Lion Brand Yarn, 3oz/ 85g skeins, each approx 125yd/113m (acrylic/polyester)

   3 skeins in #309 blue lagoon (A)

   Incredible by Lion Brand Yarn, 1¾oz/50g balls, each approx 110yd/100m (nylon)

   1 ball in #201 rainbow (B)

   Size N-P/15 (10mm) crochet hook OR SIZE TO OBTAIN GAUGE

FINISHED MEASUREMENTS

   Width at lower edge approx 58"/147.5cm

   Length 20"/50.5cm at shortest point; 36"/91cm at longest point (without fringe)

GAUGE

   7 sc and 12 rows to 4"/10cm using size N-P/15 (10mm) crochet hook.

   TAKE TIME TO CHECK YOUR GAUGE.

PONCHO

With A, ch 36.

Row 1 Work sc in 2nd ch from hook and in each ch across—35 sc. Ch 1, turn.

Row 2 Sc in each sc. Ch 1, turn.

Rep row 2 until piece measures 48"/122cm from beg. Fasten off.

FINISHING

Fold foundation chain edge to top left-hand edge, matching A to A and B to B (see schematic), and sew from A to B.

FRINGE

Cut lengths of B 8"/20.5cm long and attach in every other row or st around neck. Cut lenghts of B 16"/40.5cm long and attach in every other row or st around lower edge.

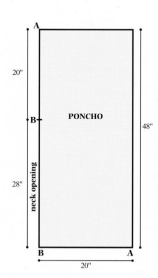

sea of love

Get ready to slow-dance—Scarlet Taylor's gorgeous capelet fastens with a ribbon at the neck for a sensual touch. "Sea of Love" appeared in the Spring/Summer '05 issue of *Family Circle Easy Knitting.*

MATERIALS

Supercotton by Schulana/Skacel Collection, 1¾oz/50g balls, each approx 98yd/90m (cotton/polyester)

  7 (8, 10, 11) balls in #5 lt blue

  One pair each sizes 9 and 10½ (5.5 and 6.5mm) needles OR SIZE TO OBTAIN GAUGE

  2yd/2m of ⅝"/16mm-wide satin ribbon

FINISHED MEASUREMENTS

  Lower edge 49½ (53½, 57½, 61½)"/125.5 (136, 146, 156)cm

  Length 16 (16½, 17½, 18½)"/40.5 (42, 44.5, 47)cm

GAUGE

  16 sts and 25 rows to 4"/10cm over St st using larger needles. TAKE TIME TO CHECK YOUR GAUGE.

BACK

With smaller needles, cast on 98 (106, 114, 122) sts.

Row 1 (RS) K2, *p2, k2; rep from * to end.

Row 2 P2, *k2, p2; rep from * to end. Rep these 2 rows for k2, p2 rib until piece measures 1"/2.5cm from beg, end with a WS row. Change to larger needles and cont in St st for 10 (10, 12, 12) rows.

Dec row (RS) K2, ssk, k to last 4 sts, k2tog, k2–96 (104, 112, 120) sts. Rep dec row every 10th (10th, 12th, 12th) row 5 times more—86 (94, 102, 110) sts. Work even until piece measures 12 (12½, 13½, 14½)"/30.5 (31.5, 34, 37)cm from beg.

SHOULDER AND NECK SHAPING

Next row (RS) K1, ssk, k to last 3 sts, k2tog, k1. Rep last row every other row 9 times more—66 (74, 82, 90) sts. Bind off 6 (7, 8, 10) sts at beg of next 4 rows, then 7 (8, 9, 9) sts at beg of next 2 rows. Bind off rem 28 (30, 32, 32) sts for back neck.

LEFT FRONT

With smaller needles cast on 50 (54, 58, 62) sts. Work in k2, p2 rib for 1"/2.5cm, dec 1 st on last row and end with a WS row—49 (53, 57, 61) sts. Change to larger needles and cont in St st for 10 (10, 12, 12) rows.

Dec row (RS) K2, ssk, k to end–48 (52, 56, 60) sts. Rep dec row every 10th (10th, 12th, 12th) row 5 times more—43 (47, 51, 55) sts. Work even until piece measures 12 (12½, 13½, 14½)"/30.5 (31.5, 34, 37)cm from beg.

SHOULDER SHAPING

Next row (RS) K1, ssk, k to end. Rep last row every other row 9 times more, then bind off 6 (7, 8, 10) sts at shoulder edge twice, then 7 (8, 9, 9) sts once, AT SAME TIME, when piece measures 13 (13½, 14½, 15½)"/33 (34, 37, 39.5)cm from beg, end with a RS row.

NECK SHAPING

Bind off 6 sts at neck edge once, then 3 (4, 5, 5) sts once.

Next row (RS) Work across to last 3 sts, k2tog, k1. Rep last row every other row 4 times more.

RIGHT FRONT

Work as for left front to dec row.

Dec row (RS) K to last 4 sts, k2tog, k2—48 (52, 56, 60) sts. Cont to work as for left front to shoulder shaping.

SHOULDER SHAPING

Next row (RS) K to last 3 sts, k2tog, k1. Rep last row every other row 9 times more, then bind off 6 (7, 8, 10) sts at shoulder edge twice, then 7 (8, 9, 9) sts once, AT SAME TIME, when piece measures same length as left front to neck shaping, end with a WS row.

NECK SHAPING

Bind off 6 sts at neck edge once, then 3 (4, 5, 5) sts once.

Next row (RS) K1, ssk, work to end. Rep last row every other row 4 times more.

POCKETS

(make 2)

With larger needles, cast on 12 sts. P next row. Cont in St st as follows:

Next row (RS) K2, M1, k to last 2 sts, M1, k1. Rep last row every other row twice more—18 sts. Work even until piece measures 2"/5cm from beg, ending with a WS row. Change to smaller needles and cont in k2, p2 rib for ½"/1.5cm. Bind off loosely in rib.

FINISHING

Sew shoulder and side seams. On each front, sew pocket 3½"/9cm from front edge and 2¼"/6cm from lower edge; as shown.

NECKBAND

With RS facing and smaller needles, pick up and k 62 (62, 66, 66) sts evenly around neck edge. Beg with row 2, work in k2, p2 rib for 3 rows.

Eyelet row (RS) Cont in rib pat as established, *work 4 sts, yo twice, work 2 sts tog; rep from * to end.

Next row Work in rib pat, dropping extra yo's from needle. Work even until band measures approx 1"/2.5cm. Bind off loosely in rib.

LEFT FRONT BAND

With RS facing and smaller needles, pick up and k 70 (70, 78, 78) sts evenly along left front edge. Beg with row 2, work in k2, p2 rib for 3 rows.

Eyelet row (RS) K2, p2, yo twice, k2tog, work to end.

Next row Work in rib pat, dropping extra yo from needle. Work even until band measures approx 1"/2.5cm. Bind off loosely in rib.

RIGHT FRONT BAND

Work as for left front to eyelet row.

Eyelet row (RS) Work in rib pat to last 6 sts, k2tog, yo twice, p2, k2. Cont to work as for left front. Weave ribbon through neckband eyelets. Trim ribbon ends to desired length.

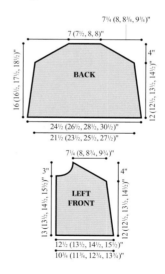

scarlet fever

Stay nice and toasty in this soft and warm alpaca shrug. The sassy red hue is a real attention-getter, but can team with lots of other colors. Designed by Veronica Manno. "Scarlet Fever" is from the Winter '04/'05 issue of *Family Circle Easy Knitting.*

MATERIALS

Worsted Weight Alpaca by Blue Sky Alpacas, 3½oz/100g balls, each approx 100yd/90m (wool/alpaca)

9 balls in #2000 red

One pair size 10 (6.5mm) needles OR SIZE TO OBTAIN GAUGE

FINISHED MEASUREMENTS

Sleeve to sleeve Approx 58"/147 cm

Length from shoulder 13"/33cm

GAUGE

14 sts and 20 rows to 4"/10cm over St st using size 10 (6.5mm) needles.

TAKE TIME TO CHECK YOUR GAUGE.

SHRUG

Cast on 98 sts. Work in garter st for 2"/5cm. Work in St st, keeping first and last 8 sts in garter st until piece measures 56"/142cm from beg, end with a WS row. Work in garter st for 2"/5cm. Bind off.

FINISHING

Block piece to measurement. Fold piece lengthwise so garter st edges meet. Sew each end for 15"/38cm to form sleeves.

paint the town

Who can resist this playful multicolor ruana stitched in cozy wool? In easy garter and stockinette stitches, you can work it up in a snap. Designed by Stitchworx, "Paint the Town" appeared in the Winter '04/'05 issue of *Family Circle Easy Knitting.*

MATERIALS

Paint Box by Classic Elite Yarns, 1¾oz/
50g balls, each approx 55yd/50m (wool)

23 balls in #6830 cobalt violet

One pair size 10½ (6.5mm) needles OR SIZE TO OBTAIN GAUGE

FINISHED MEASUREMENTS

Shoulder to shoulder 40"/101.5cm

Length from shoulder 30"/76cm

GAUGE

13 sts and 18 rows to 4"/10cm over St st using size 10½ (6.5mm) needles.

TAKE TIME TO CHECK YOUR GAUGE.

Note

Ruana is worked in 1 piece beg at back.

RUANA

Cast on 132 sts. Work in garter st for 1"/2.5cm. Beg with a RS row, work in St st, working first and last 4 sts in garter st. Work until piece measures 29½"/75cm from beg, end with a WS row.

BACK NECK

Next row (RS) Work 47 sts, work next 38 sts in garter st, work to end. Cont as established for 3 rows.

DIVIDE FOR FRONTS

Next row (RS) Work 43 sts, work 4 sts garter st, join a 2nd ball of yarn and bind off center 30 sts, work 4 sts garter st, work to end. Working both sides at once, with first and last 4 sts of each side in garter st, work even until piece measures same as back to lower edge. Work in garter st for 1"/2.5cm. Bind off.

sheer style

Get hooked on this playful poncho with its lacy peekaboo effect. Designed by Sandi Prosser, it's crocheted in subtly soft mohair and finished with flirty tassels at each corner. "Sheer Style" first appeared in the Winter '03/'04 issue of *Family Circle Easy Knitting*.

MATERIALS

Mohair Royal by Needful Yarns, Inc., 1¾oz/50g balls, each approx 235yd/215m (mohair/nylon)

- 12 balls in #10107 burgundy
- Size E/4 (3.5mm) crochet hook OR SIZE TO OBTAIN GAUGE

FINISHED MEASUREMENTS

42" x 26"/106.5 x 66cm

GAUGE

24 sts and 9 rows to 4"/10cm over pat st using size E/4 (3.5mm) hook and 2 strands of yarn held tog.
TAKE TIME TO CHECK YOUR GAUGE.

Note

Work with 2 strands of yarn held tog throughout.

Size

Poncho in one size.

STITCH GLOSSARY

tr2tog

In same st work [yo twice, draw up a lp, yo and draw through 2 lps on hook twice] twice, yo and draw through all 3 lps on hook.

triple treble (trtr)

Yo 4 times, insert hook into st, yo and draw up a lp, [yo and draw through 2 lps on hook] 5 times.

PATTERN STITCH

(multiple of 12 sts plus 11)

Row 1 (RS) Dc in 8th ch from hook, *ch 2, skip next 2 ch, dc in next ch; rep from * to end. Ch 1, turn. **Row 2** Sc in first dc, *ch 9, skip next dc, in next dc work (sc, ch 4, tr2tog), skip next dc, in next dc work (tr2tog, ch 4, sc); rep from * to last ch-2 sp, end ch 9, skip last dc, sc in 3rd ch of ch-8. **Note** On all foll row 2, sc in 3rd ch of ch-5. Ch 10 (counts as trtr and ch 4), turn. **Row 3** Sc in first ch-9 lp, *ch 4, in next tr2tog work (tr2tog, ch 4, sl st, ch 4, tr2tog), ch 4, sc in next ch-9 lp; rep from *, end ch 4, trtr in last sc. Ch 1, turn. **Row 4** Sc in trtr, *ch 5, sc in next tr2tog; rep from *, end ch 5, sc in 6th ch of ch-10. Ch 5 (counts as dc and ch 2), turn. **Row 5** Dc in first ch-5 lp, ch 2, dc in next sc, *ch 2, dc in next ch-5 lp, ch 2, dc in next sc; rep from * to end. Ch 5 (counts as dc and ch 2), turn. **Row 6** Skip first dc, dc in next dc, *ch 2, dc in next dc; rep from *, end ch 2, dc in 3rd ch of ch-5. Ch 5 (counts as dc and ch 2), turn. **Row 7** Rep row 6. Ch 1, turn.

Rep rows 2-7 for pat st.

PONCHO

Beg at front bottom edge, using 2 strands of yarn held tog, ch 263. Work rows 1-7 of pat st once, then rep rows 2 to 7 eight times and rows 2 to 5 once.

Neck opening

Next row Skip first dc, dc in next dc, [ch 2, dc in next dc] 30 times, ch 68, skip next 22 dc, dc in next dc, [ch 2, dc in next dc] 31 times, end ch 2, dc in 3rd ch of ch-5. Ch 5 (counts as dc and ch 2), turn.

Next row Skip first dc, dc in next dc, [ch 2, dc in next dc] 31 times, ch 2, [sk next 2 ch, dc in next ch, ch 2] 22 times, dc in next dc, [ch 2, dc in next dc] 30 times, end ch 2, dc in 3rd ch of ch-5. Ch 5 (counts as dc and ch 2), turn.

Next row Skip first dc, dc in next dc, *ch 2, dc in next dc; rep from *, end ch 2, dc in 3rd ch of ch-5. Ch 1, turn. Rep rows 2 to 7 of pat st 9 times, then rows 2 to 5 once. Fasten off.

FINISHING

Lightly block piece to measurements.

Edging

From RS, join 2 strands of yarn with a sl st in side of first row of front. **Row 1** Ch 5, *dc in next row, ch 2; rep from *, end dc in side of last row of back. Fasten off. Rep on opposite side edge. Make four 3½"/9cm-long tassels. Sew one to each corner of poncho, as shown.

great speckled shrug

With this marvelous mottled effect, this shrug is simple, yet oh-so-special. It gives a modern edge to most any outfit. Designed by Marcia Cleary, "Great Speckled Shrug" appeared in the Spring/Summer '05 issue of *Family Circle Easy Knitting.*

MATERIALS

Jewel Box by Caron International, 2½oz/70.9g skeins, each approx 100yd/92m (acrylic/rayon/polyester)

- 6 (6, 7) skeins in #0009 emerald
- One pair size 9 (5.5mm) needles OR SIZE TO OBTAIN GAUGE
- Size J/10 (6mm) crochet hook

FINISHED MEASUREMENTS

- From sleeve edge to sleeve edge 41 (43, 47)"/104 (109, 119.5)cm
- Sleeve width at cuff edge 10 (10, 11)"/25.5 (28, 28)cm
- Body width 26 (28, 30)"/66 (71, 76)cm

GAUGE

14 sts and 20 rows to 4"/10cm over pat st using size 9 (5.5mm) needles.

TAKE TIME TO CHECK YOUR GAUGE.

Note

Garment is worked from sleeve edge to sleeve edge.

PATTERN STITCH

Alternate 5 rows St st and 5 rows rev St st:

Row 1 (RS and beg St st section) Knit.

Row 2 Purl.

Row 3 Knit.

Row 4 Purl.

Row 5 Knit.

Row 6 (WS and beg rev St st section) Knit.

Row 7 Purl.

Row 8 Knit.

Row 9 Purl.

Row 10 Knit.

Rep rows 1-10 for pat st.

SHRUG

Cast on 36 (38, 38) sts.

FIRST SLEEVE

Work in rev St st for 16 rows. Beg pat st and inc 1 st at beg and end of rows 6, 11, 16 and 21—44 (46, 46) sts.

Rows 22 and 23 Cast on 2 sts at beg of each row—48 (50, 50) sts.

Work 2 more rows even in pat.

For size Large only Inc 1 st at beg and end of next row—52 sts. Work 4 more rows even in pat.

BODY

For all sizes Cast on 10 (12, 14) sts at beg of next 2 rows—68 (74, 80) sts. Cont to work in pat until piece measures approx 26 (28, 30)"/66 (71, 76)cm from cast-on sts for body, end with row 5 or row 10 of pat.

SECOND SLEEVE

For all sizes Bind off 10 (12, 14) sts at beg of first 2 rows of next 5-row section—48 (50, 52) sts. Work 3 rows even in pat.

For size Large only Dec 1 st at beg and end of first row of next 5-row section—50 sts. Work 4 rows even in pat.

For all sizes Bind off 2 sts at beg of first 2 rows of next 5-row section—44 (46, 46) sts. Work 3 rows even in pat. Dec 1 st at beg and end of first row of each 5-row section 4 times—36 (38, 38) sts. Cont to work in pat to correspond to first sleeve, end 16 rows rev St st. Bind off.

FINISHING

Sew underarm and sleeve seams. With RS facing, join yarn at one side seam, ch 2, work 1 rnd dc evenly around opening, join with sl st to starting ch-2. Fasten off.

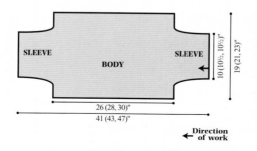

here comes treble

Packed with pizzazz, striking poncho made in triple treble crochet fuses traditional crochet with fashion-forward color motifs. Designed by Sandi Prosser, "Here Comes Treble" appeared in the Winter '04/'05 issue of *Family Circle Easy Knitting*.

MATERIALS

Merino Fine by Naturally/S.R. Kertzer, 1¾oz/50g balls, each approx 109yd/100m (wool)

- 8 balls in #227 black (D)
- 4 balls each in #230 brick red (A) and #228 brown (C)
- 3 balls in #223 white (B)
- Size I/9 (5.5mm) crochet hook OR SIZE TO OBTAIN GAUGE

FINISHED MEASUREMENTS

- Width 76"/193cm
- Length 32"/81cm (not including fringe)

GAUGE

One motif to 3½"/9cm square using size I/9 (5.5mm) crochet hook.

TAKE TIME TO CHECK YOUR GAUGE.

STITCH GLOSSARY

Triple Treble Crochet (tr tr)

Yo 4 times, insert hook into sp indicated, yo and draw up a loop, [yo, draw through 2 lps on hook] 5 times.

MOTIF 1 (make 45)

With A, ch 4. Join ch with a sl st forming a ring.

Rnd 1 (RS) Ch 3 (counts as 1 dc), work 2 dc in ring, ch 1, [work 3 dc in ring, ch 1] 3 times. Join rnd with a sl st in top of beg ch-3. Fasten off.

Rnd 2 From RS, join B with a sl st in any ch-1 sp. Ch 3 (counts as 1 dc), work (2 dc, ch 1, 3 dc) in same sp as joining (first corner made), work (3 dc, ch 1, 3 dc) in each of next 3 ch-1 sps—4 corners made. Join rnd with a sl st in top of beg ch-3. Fasten off.

MOTIF 2 (make 45)

Work as for Motif 1, using C for rnd 1 instead of A, and A for rnd 3 instead of C.

35

FINISHING

With WS facing and D, sc motifs tog foll placement diagram for back and front. Sc front and back tog along shoulder seams. Turn poncho RS out.

NECK EDGING

From RS, join D with a sl st in top of right shoulder seam.

Rnd 1 Ch 3 (counts as 1 dc), work 2 dc in same sp as joining, ch 1, *[work 3 dc in next ch-1 sp, ch 1] 3 times, work 3 dc in center of next seam ch 1; rep from * around 7 times, end [work 3 dc in next ch-1 sp, ch 1] 3 times. Join rnd with a sl st in top of beg ch-3. Fasten off.

LOWER EDGING

From RS, join D with a sl st in bottom of right shoulder seam.

Rnd 1 Ch 3 (counts as 1 dc), work 2 dc in same sp as joining, *[work 3 dc in next ch-1 sp, ch 1] 3 times, work 3 dc in center of seam, ch 1; rep from * 5 times more, [work 3 dc in next ch-1 sp, ch 1] 3 times, work 6 dc in corner ch-1 sp of front bottom point, ch 1. Cont as foll: *[work 3 dc in next ch-1 sp, ch 1] 3 times, work 3 dc in center of seam, ch 1; rep from * 12 times more, [work 3 dc in next ch-1 sp, ch 1] 3 times, work 6 dc in corner ch-1 sp of back bottom point, ch 1. Cont as foll: *[work 3 dc in next ch-1 sp, ch 1] 3 times, work 3 dc in center of seam, ch 1; rep from * 5 times more, end [work 3 dc in next ch-1 sp, ch 1] 3 times. Join rnd with a sl st in top of beg ch-3. Fasten off.

FRINGE

Cut 8"/20cm lengths of all colors. For each fringe, gather two strands of D and one strand of each rem color; fold in half. From WS, insert hook into sp between two 3-dc groups of front bottom point, then draw center of strands through forming a lp. Pull ends through this lp, then pull to tighten. Cont as foll: *skip next two 3-dc groups, attach fringe in next ch-1 sp; rep from * around, attaching a fringe into sp between two 3-dc groups of back bottom point.

TIE

With A, ch 150.

Row 1 Sl st in 2nd ch from hook and in each ch across. Fasten off. Beg and end at center front, weave tie under and over 3-dc groups of neck edging.

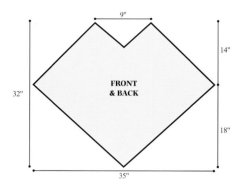

Shoulder

1	2	1	2	1		
2	1	2	1	2		
1	2	1	2	1	2	1
2	1	2	1	2	1	2
1	2	1	2	1	2	1
2	1	2	1	2	1	2
1	2	1	2	1	2	1

Shoulder

FRONT

Shoulder

		2	1	2	1	2
		1	2	1	2	1
2	1	2	1	2	1	2
1	2	1	2	1	2	1
2	1	2	1	2	1	2
1	2	1	2	1	2	1
2	1	2	1	2	1	2

Shoulder

BACK

striped for success

This poncho is made simply by sewing two rectangles together. Yet its snappy striped pattern, coupled with its fuzzy texture, lends it a luxurious feel. Designed by Kennita Tully, "Striped for Success" appeared in the Winter '04/'05 issue of *Family Circle Easy Knitting*.

MATERIALS

Frenzy by Bernat, 1¾oz/50g balls, each approx 60yd/55m (nylon/acrylic/polyester/alpaca/mohair)

   3 balls in #55040 black (MC)

   1 ball each in #55330 violet (A), #55530 red (B), #55416 lilac (C), #55134 marine (D), #55105 blue (E), #55605 orange (F) and #55415 white (G)

   One pair size 11 (8mm) needles OR SIZE TO OBTAIN GAUGE

FINISHED MEASUREMENTS

   Width (lower edge) 98"/249cm

   Length 25"/63.5

GAUGE

   10 sts and 14 rows to 4"/10cm over St st using size 11 (8mm) needles.

   TAKE TIME TO CHECK YOUR GAUGE.

Note

   Poncho is knit working 2 rectangles of equal size.

PONCHO

Rectangle 1

With A, cast on 48 sts. Working in St st, work 16 rows A, 16 rows MC, 16 rows B, 16 rows C, 16 rows MC, 16 rows D. Bind off in D.

Rectangle 2

With E, cast on 48 sts. Working in St st, *work 8 rows E, 8 rows F, 8 rows MC, 8 rows G, 8 rows MC; rep from * once more, work 8 rows E, 8 rows F. Bind off in F.

FINISHING

Sew cast-on edge of rectangle 1 to upper right edge of rectangle 2 and cast-on edge of rectangle 2 to upper right edge of rectangle 1.

keep it short

Go retro with this wide chevron-striped capelet from Sandi Prosser. With a mock turtleneck and a length that reaches just above the elbows, it's the ideal piece for when you need a light, but chic, cover-up. "Keep It Short" first appeared in the Fall '04 issue of *Family Circle Easy Knitting.*

MATERIALS

Two.Two by Classic Elite Yarns, 1¾oz/50g hanks, each approx 55yd/50m (wool)

4 hanks in #1573 olive (MC)

3 hanks each in #1504 turquoise (B) and #1592 purple (C)

Size L/11 (8mm) crochet hook OR SIZE TO OBTAIN GAUGE

FINISHED MEASUREMENTS

Width around lower edge 62"/158cm

Length from shoulder approx 14"/35.5cm

GAUGE

14 sts and 6 rows to 4"/10cm over chevron pat using size L/11 (8mm) crochet hook.

TAKE TIME TO CHECK YOUR GAUGE.

STRIPE PATTERN

8 rnds MC, 7 rnds A, 6 rnds B.

Note

Use 1 strand A and B held together throughout.

Size

Capelet in one size.

PONCHO

Neckband

Working neckband widthwise and beg at center back neck, with MC, ch 10.

Row 1 (RS) Sc in 2nd ch from hook and in each ch to end. Ch 1, turn.

Row 2 Working through back loops only, sc in each sc. Ch 1, turn. Rep row 2 until piece measures 17"/43cm from beg, end with a WS row. Fasten off. Sew last row and beg ch tog to form neckband.

BODY

With RS facing and MC, join yarn to any st at side of neckband. Ch 1, sc in same sp as joining, work 89 sc around. Join with sl st to first sc—90 sc. Cont in stripe pat as foll:

Rnds 2–4 Ch 1, 2 hdc in same sp as last sl st, *1 hdc in each of next 3 sts, draw up a lp in next 3 sts, yo and draw through all lps on hook (sc3tog), 1 hdc in each of next 3 sts, 3 hdc in next st (inc); rep from * around, end with 1 hdc in each of next 3 sts, sc3tog, 1 hdc in each of next 3 sts, 1 hdc in first st. Join with sl st in first hdc.

Rnd 5 Ch 1, 3 hdc in same sp as last sl st, *1 hdc in each of next 3 sts, sc3tog, 1 hdc in each of next 3 sts, 5 hdc in next st (inc); rep from * around, end with 1 hdc in each of next 3 sts, sc3tog, 1 hdc in each of next 3 sts, 2 hdc in first st. Join with sl st in first hdc.

Rnds 6–8 Ch 1, 2 hdc in same sp as last sl st, *1 hdc in each of next 4 sts, sc3tog, 1 hdc in each of next 4 sts, 3 hdc in next st; rep from * around, end with 1 hdc in each of next 4 sts, sc3tog, 1 hdc in each of next 4 sts, 1 hdc in first st. Join with sl st in first hdc.

Rnd 9 Ch 1, 3 hdc in same sp as last sl st, *1 hdc in each of next 4 sts, sc3tog, 1 hdc in each of next 4 sts, 5 hdc in next st (inc); rep from *, end 1 hdc in each of next 4 sts, sc3tog, 1 dc in each of next 4 sts, 2 hdc in first st. Join with sl st in first hdc.

Rnds 10–12 Ch 1, 2 hdc in same sp as last sl st, *1 hdc in each of next 5 sts, sc3tog, 1 hdc in each of next 5 sts, 3 hdc in next st; rep from *, end with 1 hdc in each of next 5 sts, sc3tog, 1 hdc in each of next 5 sts, 1 hdc in first st. Join with sl st in first hdc.

Cont in this way to inc 18 sts on the next and foll 4th rnd, until 21 rnds of stripe pat are complete.

Fasten off.

earthly delight

Basic neutrals go from dull to dynamic in this simple-yet-elegant garter stitch wrap designed by Suzan Lee. The shimmer of metallic yarn is coupled with the sheen of nylon for a sexy creation that dresses up any evening outing. "Earthly Delight" first appeared in the Holiday '04 issue of *Family Circle Easy Knitting.*

MATERIALS

Quest by Berroco, Inc, 1³⁄₄oz/50g balls, each approx 82yd/76m (nylon)

   8 balls in #9808 gold (A)

Lazer FX by Berroco, Inc, .35oz/10g balls, each approx 70yd/64m (polyester)

   7 balls in #6001 gold (B)

   One pair size 13 (9mm) needles OR SIZE TO OBTAIN GAUGE

   Crochet hook for fringe

FINISHED MEASUREMENTS

   67" x 14"/170 x 35.5cm (excluding fringe)

GAUGE

   10 sts and 27 rows to 4"/10cm over garter st using 1 strand each A and B and size 13 (9mm) needles.

   TAKE TIME TO CHECK YOUR GAUGE.

Note

   Use 1 strand A and B held together throughout.

SHAWL

With 1 strand each A and B, cast on 168 sts. Work in garter st for 14"/35.5cm. Bind off.

FINISHING

Cut 29"/73.5cm lengths of B. With crochet hook and 4 strands held together, attach fringe evenly (approx 1½"/4cm apart) along 2 short edges and 1 long edge of shawl.

in the bag

It's not what you wear that matters—it's what you carry.

li'l red bag

This trusty cabled bag, stitched in sturdy wool, is the perfect companion for a stroll through a park or a jaunt down a city street. And, better yet, it's washable! Designed by Linda Cyr, "Lil' Red Bag" first appeared in the Winter '04/'05 issue of *Family Circle Easy Knitting*.

MATERIALS

Wool-Ease Chunky by Lion Brand Yarn, 5oz/140g balls, each approx 153yd/140m (acrylic/wool)

  3 balls in #135 spice

  Size 10½ (6.5mm) circular needle, 24"/60cm long OR SIZE TO OBTAIN GAUGE

  One pair size 10½ (6.5mm) needles

  Cable needle

  Stitch marker

FINISHED MEASUREMENTS

  Approx 14"/35.5cm wide x 12"/30.5cm long (not including handles)

GAUGE

  12 sts and 20 rnds to 4"/10cm over St st using size 10½ (6.5mm) needle.

  TAKE TIME TO CHECK YOUR GAUGE.

STITCH GLOSSARY

4-st RC Sl next 2 sts to cn and hold to back, k next 2 sts, k2 from cn.

4-st LC Sl next 2 sts to cn and hold to front, k next 2 sts, k2 from cn.

6-st RC Sl next 3 sts to cn and hold to back, k next 3 sts, k3 from cn.

6-st LC Sl next 3 sts to cn and hold to front, k next 3 sts, k3 from cn.

CABLE PATTERN

Rnd 1 *K5, [p2, k9, p2, k5] 3 times; rep from * once more.

Rnd 2 *K5, [p2, 6-st RC, k3, p2, k5] 3 times; rep from * once more.

Rnds 3 and 4 Rep rnd 1.

Rnd 5 *K5, [p2, k3, 6-st LC, p2, k5] 3 times; rep from * once more.

Rnd 6 Rep rnd 1.

Rep rnds 1-6 for cable pat.

CABLE PANEL (over 14 sts)

Row 1 (RS) K3, p1, 4-st RC, k2, p1, k3.

Row 2 P3, k1, p6, k1, p3.

Row 3 K3, p1, k2, 4-st LC, p1, k3.

Row 4 Rep row 2.

Rep rows 1-4 for cable panel.

BAG

Beg at bottom edge with circular needle, cast on 118 sts. Pm and join, being careful not to twist sts. Sl marker every rnd. Beg with a k rnd, work in garter st for 6 rnds. Work in cable pat, rep rnds 1-6 eight times.

Next rnd *P5, [p2, (p1, p2tog) 3 times, p2, k5] 3 times; rep from * once more—100 sts. Beg with a k rnd, work in garter st for 4 rnds. Bind off all sts knitwise.

HANDLES (make 2)

With straight needles, cast on 14 sts. Work row 4 of cable panel. Cont to rep rows 1-4 of cable panel 18 times. Bind off.

FINISHING

Whipstitch bottom seam closed. Fold handles lengthwise so that the two St st sections meet at the center back and sew back seam of handle. Sew on handles as shown

room for squares

With this adorable satchel, toting around your essentials has never been so easy or so chic. Made of crocheted squares, it's lightweight but strong. Designed by Jacqueline van Dillen, "Room for Squares" first appeared in the Spring/Summer 2005 issue of *Family Circle Easy Knitting.*

MATERIALS

Crochet Nylon by J&P Coats/Coats & Clark, each spool approx 150yd/137m (nylon)

4 spools in #16 natural

Size G/6 (4mm) crochet hook OR SIZE TO OBTAIN GAUGE

8"/20.5cm heavy-duty zipper

Piece of lining material 12" x 25"/30.5 x 63.5cm

Sewing thread

FINISHED MEASUREMENTS

Approx 8"/20.5cm square and 1½"/4cm deep with 34"/86.5cm shoulder strap

GAUGE

5 hdc and 7 rows to 4"/10cm using size G/6 (4mm) crochet hook. Each square measures 2½"/6.5cm.

TAKE TIME TO CHECK YOUR GAUGE.

Note

1) To work 3 dc tog, (yo, insert hook, yo and draw up a lp, yo and draw through 2 lps on hook) 3 times in specified st, yo and draw through all 4 lps on hook.

2) To work 4 dc tog, (yo, insert hook, yo and draw up a lp, yo and draw through 2 lps on hook) 4 times in specified st, yo and draw through all 5 lps on hook.

BAG

Ch 7, join with sl st to form ring.

SQUARES

(make 32)

Rnd 1 Ch 2 (counts as hdc), work 15 hdc in ring, join with sl st to 2nd ch of beg ch-2.

Rnd 2 Ch 3, work 3 dc tog in sp between beg ch-2 of previous rnd and next dc, ch 1, skip 2 dc foll 3-dc-tog, *work 4 dc tog between last skipped dc and next dc, ch 1, skip 2 dc foll 3-dc tog; rep from * 6 times more, join with sl st to top of 3-dc tog.

Rnd 3 Sl st in next ch-1 sp, ch 2 (counts as hdc), work 3 hdc in same sp, *ch 3, 4 hdc in next sp, ch 1, 4 hdc in next sp; rep from * twice more, end ch 3, 4 hdc in next sp, ch 1, join with sl st to 2nd ch of beg ch-2. Fasten off.

FRONT (join 16 squares)

Rows 1 and 2 Hold 1 square behind another with WS tog. Work sc through corresponding hdc and ch-sps, working 2 sc in each corner sp. Do not fasten off. Cont to join 3 more pairs of squares in this way. Fasten off. Row 3 Join 4 squares to row 2 in same way. Row 4 Join 4 squares to row 3 in same way. Join the squares tog in the opposite direction in same way, skipping over the previous joining at intersections of squares.

BACK

Join 16 squares tog as for front.

SIDE STRIP/SHOULDER STRAP

Ch 10.

Row 1 Starting in third ch from hook, work hdc in each ch across—9 hdc, counting turning ch as hdc. Ch 2, turn.

Row 2 Skip first hdc, hdc in each hdc across. Ch 2, turn.

Rep row 2 until piece measures 60"/152cm from beg. Fasten off.

ZIPPER PLACKET (MAKE 2)

Ch 5. Work as for side strip/shoulder strap on 4 hdc until piece measures 9½"/24cm. Fasten off.

FINISHING

Sew short ends of side strip/shoulder strap tog. Place seam at center seam of one joined square and pin edge of strip around 3 sides of square. With RS of joined square facing, sc square and strip tog as pinned. Join opposite edge of strip to remaining square in same way (remainder of strip is shoulder strap). With RS of one square facing, join long edge of one zipper placket piece with sc to free edge. Rep on opposite side of bag. Sew zipper in place between plackets.

LINING

With right sides of lining facing, match 12"/30.5cm edges and fold piece in half; press guideline on fold to mark bottom edge of bag. Mark 2"/5cm above fold line on right and left edges of fabric. Bring fold line up to meet 2"/5cm mark, forming a pleat between right sides of fabric. Pin raw side edges together being sure that the pleated fabric is included. Sew sides with ½"/1.5cm seam. Press top ½"/1.5cm of top raw edge of lining toward outside. Place lining inside bag so right side of lining is in view. Sew top edge of lining to outer edge of zipper band on inside of bag.

go glam

Holiday evenings call for a little extra gleam, and this purse and scarf set have glisten galore. the mesh designs in garter stitch is light and airy, with small beads adding romantic appeal. Extra-long fringe on the scarf is ultra-chic. Designed by Mari Lynn Patrick, "Go Glam" first appeared in the Holiday '04 issue of *Family Circle Easy Knitting*.

in the bag ●●●

MATERIALS

Lamé by Needful Yarns, 1¾oz/50g balls, each approx 175yd/160m (wool/lamé)

　1 ball each in #41 grey (A) and #40 silver (B) for scarf

　2 balls each in #41 grey (A) and #40 silver (B) for handbag

Scarf

　Size H/8 (5mm) crochet hook OR SIZE TO OBTAIN GAUGE

Purse

　Size E/4 (3.5mm) crochet hook OR SIZE TO OBTAIN GAUGE

Beads for both projects

　1 container blue grey matte cubes; Japanese 4x4x4; M9605.

　2 bags (50) 6mm silver plated beads

　Both available from www.beadazzled.net

　One decorative cone bead

FINISHED MEASUREMENTS

Scarf

　2½"/6.5cm wide x 62"/157cm long

Purse

　11"/28cm wide x 9"/23cm deep

GAUGE

Scarf

　9 sts to 4"/10cm over striped pat st using size H/8 (5mm) crochet hook.

Purse

19 sts to 4"/10cm over striped pat st using size E/4 (3.5mm) crochet hook.

TAKE TIME TO CHECK YOUR GAUGE.

STRIPED PATTERN STITCH

With A, ch an even number of sts.

Row 1 (WS) With A, work 1 sc in 2nd ch from hook and in each ch to end, turn. **Row 2 (RS)** With A, ch 7 (counts as first qt), skip first 2 sc, *[yo hook] 4 times, pull up a loop in next sc, [yo and through 2 loops] 5 times for quadruple treble (qt), ch 1, skip 1 sc; rep from *, end qt in last sc, drawing B through last 2 loops on hook, turn. **Row 3** With B, ch 1, 1 sc in first qt, *then going behind the ch-1, work qt in skipped sc of row 1, 1 sc in next qt; rep from *, end 1 sc in 6th ch of ch-7, turn. **Row 4** With B, ch 1, work even in sc, drawing A through last 2 loops on hook, turn. **Row 5** With A, rep row 2, only do not change to B at end of row. **Row 6** With A, ch 1, work 1 sc in each qt and 1 sc in each ch-1 space to end, drawing B through last 2 loops on hook, turn.

Rep rows 3-6 for striped pat st.

SCARF

With size H/8 (5mm) hook and A, ch 14. Working striped pat st on 13 sts, work even for 62"/157cm, end with pat row 3. Fasten off.

FRINGE

Onto one ball of color A yarn, string beads as foll: [1 silver bead, 1 grey bead] 32 times. Onto one ball of color B yarn, string beads as foll: [1 silver bead, 1 grey bead] 24 times. Then work chain st fringe in B at one end of scarf as foll: Working with size E/4 (3.5mm) hook and B, ch 1, slide first bead in place and ch 3, and cont in this way until there are 8 beads, join to end st of scarf, ch 25 and fasten off. Hook 3 more double chain fringe in B (one with beads, one without) evenly spaced to end, then using A, work 3 double chain fringe between each B fringe. Knot tightly at ends and trim carefully. Work other end's fringe in same way.

PURSE

Front

With size E/4 (3.5mm) hook and A, ch 48. Work 1 row sc—47 sts. Work in striped pat st as foll: **Next row** Inc 1 qt and ch 1 at beg and end of row. Work 1 row even on 49 sts. **Next row** Work 2 sc at beg and end of row—51 sts. **Next row** Work 2 sc at beg and end of row—53 sts. Working even in striped pat (on 27A and 26B qt sts) until there are 13 rows from beg. Dec 1 sc each end of next row then every 4th row (an sc row) twice more—47 sts or 24A and 23B qt sts. Work even until there are 7 reps of pat. Fasten off.

BACK

Work as for front for a total of 10 reps of pat. Dec 2 sts each side of next 4 rows. Fasten off.

FINISHING

With size E/4 (3.5mm) hook and B, having front and back of bag pieces with WS tog, join sides of bag through both thicknesses as foll: beg at top edge of front and matching back before flap, *work 2 sc in the 2 sc rows, ch 4 and skip the qt; rep from * to lower edge, across lower edge work 1 sc in each B qt (not in the A qt sts), then rep from * along other side of bag; then cont across inside top of front, work 1 sl st at approx ¼"/.5cm from top in every other qt in A (to draw edge in firmly), then work around flap in same way ONLY work 1 sc in each sc along the straight edge of flap; then cont for strap, work as foll: using double strand of B, ch 175 (for strap), join to opposite inside corner of bag; ch 1, then working 2-color chain st into the ch strap, work as foll: *with 2 strands B, work 1 hdc in next ch, with 2 strands A, work 1 hdc in next ch; cont in this way all along chain strap. Fasten off. With single strand B, work 1 sc in each sc and 3 sc in each ch-4 space around bag edges, then ch 1 but do not turn, work 1 backwards sc in each sc. Fasten off. For chain closure, string 8 beads alternately onto A yarn. Fasten to center of flap, winding yarn several times to fasten securely (see photo). At opposite end, join cone bead to complete chain closure. Fasten securely and cut ends carefully.

bead and vine

Tuck away the essentials in this vine-patterned purse by Ellen Lesperance. A baubled strap is a lively touch. "Bead and Vine" first appeared in the Spring/Summer '00 issue of *Family Circle Easy Knitting*.

MATERIALS

Cotton Connection D.K. No. 6 by Naturally/S.R. Kertzer, Ltd., 1¾oz/50g balls, each approx 110yd/100m (linen/cotton/wool)

1 ball in #06 natural

One pair size 6 (4mm) needles OR SIZE TO OBTAIN

Cable needle (cn)

Purchased strap

FINISHED MEASUREMENTS

- Length (closed) 6¼"/16cm
- Width 6½"/16.5cm

GAUGE

22 sts and 30 rows to 4"/10cm over St st using size 6 (4mm) needles.

TAKE TIME TO CHECK YOUR GAUGE.

STITCH GLOSSARY

RC
Sl 1 st to cn and hold to back, k1, k1 from cn.

LC
Sl 1 st to cn and hold to front, k1, k1 from cn.

RPC
Sl 1 st to cn and hold to back, k1, p1 from cn.

LPC
Sl 1 st to cn and hold to front, p1, k1 from cn.

RP2C
Sl 1 st to cn and hold to back, p1, p1 from cn.

LP2C
Sl 1 st to cn and hold to front, p1, p1 from cn.

CENTER PANEL PATTERN

(Panel of 18 sts)

Row 1 (WS) K2, p3, k3, p4, RP2C, k4.

Row 2 P3, RC, k1, RPC, k2, p3, LPC, k1, p2.

Row 3 K2, p2, k4, p2, k1, p3, RP2C, k2.

Row 4 P2, k3, RPC, p1, k1, LC, p3, LPC, p2.

Row 5 K6, LP2C, p2, k2, p4, k2.

Row 6 P2, k2, RPC, p2, k1, [LC] twice, p5.

Row 7 K4, LP2C, p4, k3, p3, k2.

Row 8 P2, k1, RPC, p3, k2, LPC, k1, LC, p3.

Row 9 K2, LP2C, p3, k1, p2, k4, p2, k2.

Row 10 P2, RPC, p3, RC, k1, p1, LPC, k3, p2.

Row 11 K2, p4, k2, p2, RP2C, k6.

Row 12 P5, [RC] twice, k1, p2, LPC, k2, p2.

Rep rows 1-12 for center panel pat.

BACK

With MC, cast on 48 sts. **Row 1 (WS)** K14, p1, work 18 sts in center panel pat, p1, k14. **Row 2 (RS)** P14, k1, work 18 sts in center panel pat, k1, p14. Cont in pat as established until piece measures 6"/15cm from beg. Bind off.

FRONT

Work as for back.

FLAP

Work as for back until piece measures 3"/7.5cm from beg. Bind off.

FINISHING

Sew side seams. Sew bind off edge off flap to bind off edge of back.

STRAP

Sew on purchased strap.

plum perfect

A drawstring bag is an accessory that no woman should be without! An additional button closure keeps your valuables safe from spillage in this smart design by Linda Cyr. "Plum Perfect" first appeared in the Winter '04/'05 issue of *Family Circle Easy Knitting*.

MATERIALS

TLC Essentials by Coats & Clark, 6oz/170g balls, each approx 326yd/299m (acrylic)

- 2 balls in #2533 dark plum
- One pair size 7 (4.5mm) needles OR SIZE TO OBTAIN GAUGE
- Size 7 (4.5mm) circular needle, 29"/74cm long
- Two size 9 (5.5mm) dpn for I-cord straps
- Crochet hook size 7 (4.5mm)
- Stitch marker
- One 1⅝"/41mm toggle button

FINISHED MEASUREMENTS

Approx 10"/25.5cm wide x 14"/35.5cm long x 6"/15 deep (not including straps)

GAUGE

16 sts and 24 rows to 4"/10cm over St st using size 7 (4.5mm) needles.

TAKE TIME TO CHECK YOUR GAUGE.

BAG

Bottom

With straight needles, cast on 40 sts.

Rows 1-48 Sl 1, k to end.

Change to circular needle.

Row 49 Sl 1, k to end.

SIDES

Pick up and k24 sts evenly spaced across side edge of bottom, 40 sts across cast-on edge, 24 sts across opposite side edge—88 sts. Join, mark end of rnd and sl marker every rnd.

BOTTOM BORDER

Beg with a p rnd, work in garter st for 10 rnds. Cont in St st and work even for 12"/30.5cm.

TOP BORDER

Beg with a p rnd, work in garter st for 7 rnds. Next rnd K to within 4 sts of marker, turn. Change to straight needles.

FLAP

Rows 1–46 Wyif, sl 1 purlwise, wyib, k31. Note Leave rem sts on circular needle.

BUTTON LOOP

Bind off first 16 sts, place st from RH needle onto crochet hook, ch 8 (for button loop), place st from crochet hook back onto RH needle, cont to bind off rem sts.

LEFT DRAWSTRING CASING

From RS, with straight needles, join yarn in next st after flap (4 sts before st marker), k46, dropping marker, leave rem sts on circular needle. Rows 1-9 Wyif, sl 1 purlwise, wyib, k45. Bind off.

RIGHT DRAWSTRING CASING

From RS, with straight needles, join yarn in next st after left drawstring casing, bind off next 4 sts, k to end—46 sts. **Rows 1–9** Wyif, sl 1 purlwise, wyib, k45. Bind off.

POCKET

With straight needles, cast on 20 sts.

Rows 1–7 Wyif, sl 1 purlwise, wyib, k19.

Rows 8, 10, 12, 14, 16, 18, 20, 22, 24 and 26 Wyif, sl 1 purlwise, wyib, k3, p12, k4.

Rows 9, 11, 13, 15, 17, 19, 21, 23, 25 and 27 (RS) Rep row 1.

Row 28 Wyif, sl 1 purlwise, wyib, k7, k2tog, yo, ssk, k8—19 sts.

Row 29 Wyif, sl 1 purlwise, wyib, k9, work (k1, p1) in yo, k9—20 sts.

Rows 30 and 31 Rep row 1. Bind off.

I-CORD STRAPS

With dpn and 2 strands of yarn held tog, cast on 4 sts. Work in I-cord as foll: *Next row (RS)** With 2nd dpn, k4, do not turn. Slide sts back to beg of needle to work next row from RS; rep from * until I-cord measures 50"/127cm from beg. Cut yarns leaving long tails. Thread tails into tapestry needle and weave through sts. Pull tight to gather; fasten off securely.

FINISHING

Sew pocket to front of bag so bottom edge is 2½"/6.5cm above bottom border and it is centered side to side. Fold each drawstring casing over to RS so bottom edge is even with first garter st ridge of top border; sew in place. With front of bag facing, insert a strap end through a drawstring casing and draw through to back of backpack. Sew ends of straps to bottom back corners. To adjust straps and gather opening closed, tie excess strap at center front in an overhand knot. Sew toggle to front of backpack, centering it under pocket buttonhole.

beyond basics

Judi Alweil uses garter stitch to create a bag that's more elementary than it appears. Cap it off with festive fringe and crocheted handles, and the result? A summery delight. "Beyond Basics" first appeared in the Spring/Summer '00 issue of *Family Circle Easy Knitting.*

MATERIALS

Rafia by Judi & Co., 1¾oz/50g balls, each approx 72yds/65m (raffia)

- 2 balls in white
- Size 7 (4.5mm) circular needle, 16"/40cm long OR SIZE TO OBTAIN GAUGE
- Size D3 (3mm) crochet hook
- Two pearlized pony beads
- Two 4"/10cm diameter metal rings
- Lining fabric (optional)

FINISHED MEASUREMENTS

8"/20.5cm wide by 6¾"/17cm tall (from under the handle)

GAUGE

18 sts and 36 rows to 4"/10cm using size 7 (4.5mm) needle. TAKE TIME TO CHECK YOUR GAUGE.

BAG (make 2 pieces)

With crochet hook, work 82 sc tightly around ring to cover. Join with sl st, ch 1, turn. **Rnd 1** Sc in each of next 28 sts. With circular needle, pick up 28 sts along sc just worked. K 1 row. Cont in garter st, inc 1 st each side every other row 5 times—38 sts. Work even until piece measures 6¾"/17cm from top. Bind off.

FINISHING

Sl st bottom and sides tog on WS up to last inc, leaving approx 1½"/4cm opening at the top of each side.

FRINGE

Cut 26 strands each 4"/10cm long. Fold strands in half. With crochet hook, loop raffia through raised row under ring and make a knot. Rep across row.

BAG TIES

Attach raffia to center of one side of bag opening. Ch approx 8"/20.5cm and fasten off. Pull tie through hole of bead. Knot end.

winter brights

Add some vivid color to an otherwise muted season with this jazzy zigzag backpack designed by Norah Gaughan. Completed in the round with a drawstring pompom closure at the top, it's a refreshing alternative to the average drab shoulder sack. "Winter Brights" first appeared in the Winter '99/'00 issue of *Family Circle Easy Knitting*.

MATERIALS

Harvest by JCA/Reynolds, 1¾oz/50g balls, each approx 120yd/110m (wool)

   2 ball in #429 berry (A)

   Signature Eternity, 1¾oz/50g balls, each approx 220yd/81m (acrylic/wool)

   1 ball each in #84 pink (B), #68 crimson (C) and #83 azalea (D)

Dover, 13/4oz/50g balls, each approx 83yd/76m (wool)

   1 ball in #8 purple (E)

   Size 7 (4.5mm) circular needle, 24"/60cm long OR SIZE TO OBTAIN GAUGE

   Two size 7 (4.5mm) dpn

   Stitch marker

   6"/15.5cm square of cardboard (for bottom)

FINISHED MEASUREMENTS

   Circumference 24"/60cm

GAUGE

   20 sts and 22 rows to 4"/10cm in St st and chart pat using size 7 (4.5mm) needles.

   TAKE TIME TO CHECK YOUR GAUGE.

BACKPACK

With A, beg at lower edge, cast on 120 sts. Join, being careful not to twist sts on needle. Mark end of rnd and sl marker every rnd. Work in rnds of St st and chart pat until 30 rows of chart have been worked twice, then work rnds 1-16 once more.

Next rnd Cont in chart pat, [k2tog, yo twice, ssk, k11] 8 times. On next rnd, work 2 sts in each double yo. Work even through chart rnd 30. P next rnd for turning ridge. Cont in St st for 2"/5cm more. Bind off. Fold top edge to inside at turning ridge and sew in place.

FINISHING

Lay bag on table so that front and back eyelet are aligned. Sew bottom edge of bag tog. Turn inside out. Punch hole in each corner of cardboard square. Center cardboard on bottom edge and bring the ends of the seam tog over cardboard and fasten. Return to RS.

I-cord

With dpn and C, cast on 3 sts. Do not turn. *Sl sts to beg of needle and bring yarn around from back and k3. Rep from * for I-cord for approx 60"/152.5cm. Bind off. Knot one end of I-cord and thread through back corner of bag (through hole in cardboard inside). Thread in and out of eyelets and through other back corner. Knot the end.

Make a multicolored pompom and attach to one end of I-cord. Remove cardboard before washing.

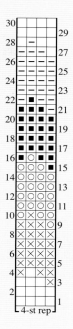

L─ 4-st rep ─⅃

Color Key

☐ Berry (A)

☒ Pink (B)

◯ Crimson (C)

■ Azalea (D)

─ Purple (E)

tutti fruitti

Sherbet-flavored shoulder bags are a cheery addition to your accessories cache. Knit in stockinette stitch, these color-banded cuties come in a small and a large size. "Tutti Fruitti" first appeared in the Spring/Summer '02 issue of _Family Circle Easy Knitting_.

MATERIALS

Microspun by Lion Brand Yarn Co., 2½oz/70g balls, each approx 168yd/154m (microfiber)

- 1 ball each in #186 orange (A), #113 red (B), #103 coral (C) and #146 fuchsia (D) for both bags
- One pair size 6 (4mm) needles OR SIZE TO OBTAIN GAUGE
- Size 6 (4mm) circular needle, 36"/92cm long
- Size E/4 (3.5mm) crochet hook
- Large plastic snap closure

FINISHED MEASUREMENTS

Small bag 8½"/21.5cm wide x 8"/20.5cm long

Large bag 11½"/29cm wide x 9"/23cm long with 3"/7.5cm gusset

GAUGE

22 sts and 30 rows to 4"/10cm over St st using size 6 (4mm) needles.

TAKE TIME TO CHECK YOUR GAUGE.

SMALL BAG

Stripe Pattern

Working in St st, work 6 rows A, *2 rows B, 1 row C, 2 rows B*, 6 rows A; rep between *'s once, [6 rows D; rep between *'s once] twice, 6 rows A; rep between *'s once, 6 rows A. These 61 rows form stripe pat.

BACK OR FRONT

(make 2 identical pieces)

Beg at lower edge with A, cast on 36 sts. Working in stripe pat, work 1 row even, then inc 1 st each side every row 6 times—48 sts. Work even in stripe pat until all 61 rows are completed. K next row on WS for turning ridge. Cont in St st with A for 6 rows more. Bind off.

FINISHING

Block pieces lightly to measurements. With circular needle and B, beg just below turning ridge at top, pick up and k 122 sts evenly around 3 edges of back piece. Bind off knitwise on **WS**. Sew front to back underneath edge in B, leaving one side seam open. Fold facing to **WS** at turning ridge and with circular needle and B, pick up and k 1 st in each st along top turning ridge. Bind off knitwise. Sew other seam of bag.

Strap

With crochet hook and B, ch 164. Work 1 sl st in each ch. Join strap to inside of bag tacking firmly for 1"/2.5cm to secure. Sew snap to inside center to close.

LARGE BAG

Note Front of bag is worked with lower gusset and back is worked with side gussets.

STRIPE PATTERN

Working in St st, *work 7 rows D, 5 rows A, 2 rows C, 5 rows B, 2 rows C; rep from * (21 rows) for stripe pat.

FRONT

Beg at lower edge with D, cast on 43 sts. Working in stripe pat, work 1 row even, then inc 1 st each side every row 6 times—55 sts. Work even through row 20 of first stripe rep. **Next row (RS)** With C, purl across for gusset pick-up ridge. Then resume 21-row stripe pat in St st and cont until 10 rows are worked after ridge. **Dec row (RS)** K2, SKP, k to last 4 sts, k2tog, k2. Rep dec row every 20th row once, every 18th row once—49 sts. Work even until 3 complete 21-row reps are worked. **Next row (WS)** With D, knit across for hem pick-up ridge. Then cont with D for 6 rows more. Bind off.

BACK

Beg at lower edge with D, cast on 71 sts. Working in stripe pat, work 1 row even, then inc 1 st each side every row 6 times—83 sts. Work even for 3 rows. **Dec row (RS)** K2, SKP, k to last 4 sts, k2tog, k2. Rep dec row every 14th row 3 times more—75 sts. Work even until 3 complete 21-row reps are worked. **Next row (WS)** With D, knit across for hem pick-up ridge. Then cont with D for 6 rows more. Bind off.

FINISHING

Block pieces lightly to measurements. With RS facing and B, pick up and k 43 sts along lower gusset ridge. Bind off knitwise on WS. With RS facing, circular needle and B, pick up and k a total of 151 sts along side and around lower edge of back. Bind off knitwise on WS. Pin front and back pieces tog, with back curving at lower gusset. Sew 2 seams of back to front, leaving 3rd seam open. With circular needle and B, pick up and k 122 sts evenly along top hem ridge. Bind off knitwise on WS. Sew other seam closed.

STRAP

With crochet hook and B, ch 176. **Row 1** Sc in 2nd ch from hook and in each ch across. Ch 4, turn. **Row 2** Working in back lps only, work 1 tr in each sc to end. Ch 1, turn. **Row 3** Working in front lps only, work 1 sc in each tr to end. Fasten off. Sew strap to outside along gusset edges tacking down for 2"/5cm on all sides of straps.

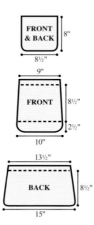

half moon

Petite but perky, this multicolored shoulder satchel will add sparkle to even the dreariest of winters. Stitched in hand-dyed yarn and tied with a silk ribbon, the croissant shape is a knockout. Designed by Miriam Gold, "Half Moon" first appeared in the Winter '04/'05 issue of *Family Circle Easy Knitting*.

MATERIALS

Shimmer Five by Colinette/Unique Kolours, 3½oz/100g balls, each approx 52yd/48m (wool/viscose)

   3 balls in #055 toscana

   One pair size 9 (5.5mm) needles OR SIZE TO OBTAIN GAUGE

   46"/117cm ribbon, 2"/5cm wide

FINISHED MEASUREMENTS

   Approx 13" x 8"/33 x 20.5cm

GAUGE

   11 sts and 16 rows to 4"/10cm over St st using size 9 (5.5mm) needles.

   TAKE TIME TO CHECK YOUR GAUGE.

BAG BACK AND FRONT

(make 2 sides alike)

Cast on 21 sts. Work in St st for 2 rows. Inc 1 st each side on next row, then every other row 7 times more—37 sts. Work even until piece measures 8"/20.5cm from beg. Bind off.

GUSSET AND HANDLE

Cast on 6 sts. Slipping first st of every row, work in St st for 38"/96.5cm. Bind off.

FINISHING

Sew cast-on and bound-off edges of gusset/handle together to form a loop. With seam at bottom, sew front and back pieces to side edges of loop, creating a gusset at the sides with the rem length at top for the handle. Seam entire length of handle to form a roll.

Pull ribbon through top center of front and back sides. Tie at top for closure.

patchwork perfect

When you crave a purse that is small and sweet, let this compact handbag, accented with a decorative seam and tassel, save the day. Designed by Linda Cyr, "Patchwork Perfect" first appeared in the Winter '04/'05 issue of *Family Circle Easy Knitting.*

MATERIALS

Lopi by Reynolds/JCA Yarns, 3½oz/100g balls, each approx 109yd/100m (wool)

  1 ball each in #212 lt green (A), #104 salmon (B) and #87 brown (C)

  One pair size 8 (5mm) needles OR SIZE TO OBTAIN GAUGE

  14"/35cm metal zipper

  Matching and contrasting sewing threads

  Sewing needle

FINISHED MEASUREMENTS

  Approx 14"/35.5cm wide x 5"/12.5cm long x 4"/10cm deep

GAUGE

  16 sts and 22 rows to 4"/10cm over St st using size 8 (5mm) needles.

  TAKE TIME TO CHECK YOUR GAUGE.

Note

  When changing colors, twist yarn on WS to prevent holes.

SIDES

(make 2)

MOTIF A

With A, cast on 14 sts. Work in St st for 22 rows. Bind off.

MOTIF B

With RS facing and B, pick up and k16 sts evenly spaced along RH edge of motif A. Beg with a p row, work in St st for 27 rows.

BEG COLOR PAT

Row 1 (RS) With C, k1, with B, k15.

Row 2 With B, p14, with C, p2.

Row 3 With C, k3, with B, k13.

Row 4 With B, p12, with C, p4.

Row 5 With C, k5, with B, k11.

Row 6 With B, p10, with C, p6. Cont to work 1 more C st every row, AT SAME TIME, when 10 rows have been completed, pm at beg of next row. Work until all sts are in C, end with a WS row. Cont in St st for 14 rows. Bind off.

MOTIF C

With RS facing and C, pick up and k16 sts evenly spaced along cast-on edge of motif A, 28 sts to marker, with A, pick up and k14 sts to end—58 sts.

BEG COLOR PAT

Row 1 (WS) With A, p13, with C, p45.

Row 2 With C, k46, with A, k12.

Row 3 With A, p11, with C, p47.

Row 4 With C, k48, with A, k10.

Row 5 With A, p9, with C, p49. Bind off for bottom edge.

GUSSET

With C, cast on 4 sts. Work in St st for 6 rows.

SIDE SHAPING

Inc row (**RS**) K1, M1, knit to last st, M1, k1—6 sts. Rep inc row every 6th row 4 times more—14 sts. Cont in St st for 68 rows.

Dec row (**RS**) Ssk, k to last 2 sts, k2tog. Rep dec row every 6th row 4 times more—4 sts. Cont in St st for 6 rows. Bind off.

FINISHING

Steam block pieces. Using contrasting thread, baste zipper to top edges of sides. Sew zipper in place using matching threads. Using thread, sew edges above and below zipper closed. Using B and overcast stitch, sew sides to gusset. Steam block seams to flatten and round corners. Remove basting sts.

SHOULDER STRAP

Cut six 60"/153cm strands of C. Draw ends to inside of bag at top side edge of gusset. On inside of bag, tie ends in a firm overhand knot. On outside of bag, tie ends in a firm overhand knot close to bag. Braid pairs of strands tog for 40"/101.5cm. Tie ends in a firm overhand knot. Draw ends to inside of bag at opposite top side edge of gusset. On inside of bag, tie ends in a firm overhand knot close to bag. Trim off excess strands.

TASSEL

Cut three 10"/25.5cm strands of B. Thread strands through hole in zipper pull. With ends of strands even, tie in an overhand knot close to bottom edge of zipper pull. Trim tassel to desired length.

know when to tote 'em

One of the most traditional carryalls around gets retooled in this clever Victoria Hilditch design. Start from the bottom up, make the straps separately, create a sturdy fabric by felting it, and *voila*! You've got an indestructible—and ingenious—knitted bag. "Know When to Tote 'Em" first appeared in the Holiday '04 issue of *Family Circle Easy Knitting.*

MATERIALS

Lamb's Pride Worsted by Brown Sheep Yarn Company, 4oz/113g balls, each approx 190yd/178m (wool/mohair)

- 6 balls in #M10 cream (MC)
- 2 balls in #M180 ruby red (CC)
- One pair size 10½ (6.5mm) needles OR SIZE TO OBTAIN GAUGE
- Size 10½ (6.5mm) circular needle, 29"/74cm long
- Size K/10½ (6.5mm) crochet hook
- Stitch holders
- Stitch marker

FINISHED MEASUREMENTS

Approx 18"/45.5cm wide x 12"/30.5cm tall (after felting)

GAUGE

12 sts and 18 rows to 4"/10cm over St st using MC and size 10½ (6.5mm) needles before felting.

16 sts and 32 rows to 4"/10cm over St st using MC and size 10½ (6.5mm) needles after felting.

TAKE TIME TO CHECK YOUR GAUGE.

TOTE

Beg at bottom, with straight needles and CC, cast on 74 sts. Work in garter st until piece measures 9"/23cm from beg. Bind off all sts loosely.

Sides

From RS with circular needle and CC, pick up and k28 sts evenly spaced along short edge of bottom, 74 sts from long edge, 28 sts from short edge and k74 sts from long edge—204 sts. Mark end of rnd and sl marker every rnd.

Next rnd Purl.

Next rnd K28, sl 1, k72, sl 1, k28, sl 1, k 72, sl 1. Rep last 2 rnds 4 times more. Change to MC.

Strap placement

Next rnd K45, place next 6 sts on a holder, cast on 6 sts, k28, place next 6 sts on a holder, cast on 6 sts, k62, place next 6 sts on a holder, cast on 6 sts, k28, place next 6 sts on a holder, cast on 6 sts, k17—204 sts.

Next rnd K28, *sl 1, k16, p1, k4, p1, k28, p1, k4, p1, k16, sl 1*, k28, rep between *'s once more.

Next rnd K45, p1, k4, p1, k28, p1, k4, p1, k62, p1, k4, p1, k28, p1, k4, p1, k17. Rep last 2 rnds 43 times more. Bind off all sts loosely.

Edging

From RS with crochet hook, join MC with a sl st in any st.

Rnd 1 Ch 1, sc in each st around. Join rnd with a sl st in first st. Fasten off.

Straps

From RS, place 6 sts from a holder onto a straight needle. Join CC and work even in garter st until piece measures same length as height of tote (without stretching). Cont to work in garter st for 82 more rows. Place sts on a holder. Work other strap on same side of bag. With WS of straps tog, sl sts from holders onto straight needles. With circular needle, and strap sts parallel, k 1 st from back needle with 1 st from front needle and bind off while working tog for three-needle bind off. Rep on opposite side of tote.

FINISHING

On WS, sew MC cast-on sts to last rnd of CC using CC. Taking care not to stretch straps, sew to sides of tote centering them between p-st guidelines.

Felting

Fill washing machine to low water setting at a hot temperature. Add a small amount of a gentle detergent. Add tote and also a pair of jeans to provide abrasion and balanced agitation. Use 15-20 minute wash cycle, including cold rinse and spin. Check measurements of tote. If it's still larger than finished measurements, repeat process with progressively shorter cycles, measuring every few minutes until measurements are achieved. Air dry or machine-dry on a low setting.

chill chasers

Why hide inside when you can stay warm in the outdoors—and look great doing it?

the twist

In anticipation of spring, this pastel troika from the Cleckheaton Design Studio picks up the lovely lavenders of April posies. Cables create a comfy cap while also dressing up the matching gloves and scarf. "The Twist" first appeared in the Winter '99/'00 issue of *Family Circle Easy Knitting*.

MATERIALS

Cleckheaton Country 8 ply by Plymouth, 1¾oz/50g balls, each approx 105yd/96m (wool) in #1980 lilac

Hat

    2 balls

Scarf

    6 balls

Gloves

    2 balls

    One pair size 6 (4mm) needles OR SIZE TO OBTAIN GAUGE

    One set size 6 (4mm) dpn

    Cable needle

FINISHED MEASUREMENTS

Hat

    Head circumference 22"/56cm

Scarf

    Width 8"/20cm

    Length 63"/160cm

GAUGE

    22 sts and 30 rows to 4"/10cm over St st using size 6 (4mm) needles.

STITCHES USED

C7B

Sl 4 sts to cn and hold to back, k3, k4 from cn.

C6B

Sl 3 sts to cn and hold to back, k3, k3 from cn.

C5B

Sl 3 sts to cn and hold to back, k2, k3 from cn.

C4B

Sl 2 sts to cn and hold to back, k2, k2 from cn.

HAT

Cast on 110 sts. Divide sts evenly onto 3 dpn. Join, taking care not to twist sts. Mark end of rnd and sl marker every rnd. P 3 rnds, inc 16 sts evenly across last rnd—126 sts.

Beg cable pat

Rnds 1–4 *P2, k7; rep from * around.

Rnd 5 *P2, C7B; rep from * around.

Rnds 6–8 Rep rnd 1.

Rep rnds 1-8 for 42 rnds more.

Shape crown

Rnd 1 *P2, k2tog, k5; rep from * around—112 sts.

Rnd 2 *P2, C6B; rep from * around.

Rnd 3 *P2, k6; rep from * around.

Rnd 4 *P2, k2tog, k4; rep from * around—98 sts.

Rnd 5 *P2, k5; rep from * around.

Rnd 6 *P2tog, k5; rep from * around—84 sts.

Rnd 7 *P1, k5; rep from * around.

Rnd 8 *P1, C5B; rep from * around.

Rnd 9 *P1, k2tog, k3; rep from * around—70 sts.

Rnd 10 *P1, k4; rep from * around.

Rnd 11 *K2tog, k3; rep from * around—56 sts.

Rnd 12 and every other rnd Knit.

Rnd 13 *K2tog, k2; rep from * around—42 sts.

Rnd 15 *K2tog, k1; rep from * around—28 sts.

Rnd 17 K2tog around—14 sts.

Rnd 19 K2tog around—7 sts.

Break yarn, thread through rem sts, draw up and fasten off securely.

SCARF

Cast on 56 sts. K 1 row, p 1 row, k 1 row, inc 14 sts evenly across last row—70 sts.

Beg edge pat

Row 1 (RS) *K6, p2; rep from * to last 6 sts, k6.

Rows 2–4 K the knit sts and p the purl sts. **Row 5** *C6B, p2; rep from * to last 6 sts, C6B.

Rows 6–8 Rep row 2.

Rep rows 1-8 for pat for 15 rows more.

Next row (WS) Work 8 sts, [p2tog p2] 5 times, p2tog, work 10 sts, p2tog, [p2tog, p2] 5 times, work 8 sts—58 sts.

Beg main pat

Row 1 K6, p2, k16, p2, k6, p2, k16, p2, k6. **Rows 2–4** K the knit sts and p the purl sts.

Row 5 C6B, p2, k16, p2, C6B, p2, k16, p2, C6B.

Rows 6–8 Rep row 2.

Rep rows 1-8 for pat until piece measures approx 59"/151cm from beg, end with row 7.

Next row (WS) Work 8 sts [inc in next st, p2] 5 times, inc in next st, work 10 sts, inc in next st [inc in next st, p2] 5 times, work 8 sts—70 sts. Work 24 rows of edge pat as before, dec 14 sts evenly across last row—56 sts. Work 3 rows rev St st. Bind off loosely knitwise.

GLOVES

Right Glove

Cast on 42 sts. K 1 row, p 1 row, k 1 row, inc 16 sts evenly across last row—58 sts.

Beg pat

Row 1 (RS) P2, *k6, p2; rep from * to end. **Rows 2–4** K the knit sts and p the purl sts.

Row 5 P2, *C6B, p2; rep from * to end.

Rows 6–8 Rep row 2.

Rep rows 1-8 for pat for 16 rows more, dec 13 sts evenly across last row—45 sts. Cont to work all sts in St st as foll: Work 2 rows even.**

Beg hand shaping

Next row (RS) K25, inc in next st, k1, inc in next st, k17—47 sts. Work 3 rows even. **Next row** K25, inc in next st, k3, inc in next st, k17—49 sts. Work 3 rows even.

Next row K25, inc in next st, k5, inc in next st, k17—51 sts. Work 3 rows even.

Next row K25, inc in next st, k7, inc in next st, k17—53 sts. P 1 row.

Thumb shaping

Next row K38, turn. **Next row** P12, turn, cast on 3 sts—15 sts.*** Work 16 rows on these 15 sts.

Top shaping

Row 1 *K1, k2tog; rep from * to end—10 sts.

Row 2 Purl.

Row 3 K2tog across—5 sts. Break yarn, run through rem sts and fasten off. With RS facing, pick up and k 3 sts from cast on sts at base of thumb, k to end—44 sts. Work 11 rows even, dec 2 sts evenly across last row—42 sts.

Index finger

Next row K27, turn.

Next row P12, turn, cast on 2 sts.***

Work 20 rows on these 14 sts.

Top shaping

Row 1 K2tog across—7 sts.

Row 2 Purl.

Row 3 K1, *k2tog; rep from * to end—4 sts. Break yarn, run through rem sts and fasten off.

Middle finger

With RS facing, join yarn and pick up and k 2 sts from cast-on sts at base of index finger, k5, turn.

Next row P12, turn, cast on 2 sts.

Work 24 rows on these 14 sts.

Top shaping

Work as for index finger.

Ring finger

With RS facing, join yarn and pick up and k 2 sts from cast-on sts at base of middle finger, k5, turn.

Next row P12, turn, cast on 2 sts.

Complete as for index finger from *** to end.

Little finger

With RS facing, join yarn and pick up and k 2 sts from cast-on sts at base of ring finger, k5, turn.

Next row P12.

Work 12 rows on these 12 sts.

Top shaping

Next row *K2tog; rep from * to end—6 sts.

Next Row *P2tog; rep from * to end—3 sts.

Break off yarn, run through rem sts, draw up and fasten off securely.

Left Glove

Work to correspond to Right Glove, reversing placement of thumb and fingers. Beg hand shaping as foll:

Next row K17, inc in next st, K1, inc in next st, k25—47 sts.

FINISHING

Sew thumb, fingers and side seams.

a bit fuzzy

Lisa Ventry's faux-fur boa is simply stunning and utterly luxe. Just cast on, knit in stockinette stitch to desired length, and it's yours. "A Bit Fuzzy" first appeared in the Winter '02 issue of *Family Circle Easy Knitting.*

MATERIALS

Fun Furs by Brand yarn, 1¾oz/50g balls, each approx 64yds/58m (polyester)

 4 balls in #20 white

 One pair size 10 (6mm) needles OR SIZE TO OBTAIN GAUGE

FINISHED MEASUREMENTS

 Approx 9" x 66"/23 x 167.5cm

GAUGE

 18 sts and 20 rows to 4"/10cm over St st using size 10 (6mm) needles.

 TAKE TIME TO CHECK YOUR GAUGE.

SCARF

Cast on 40 sts. Work in St st until piece measures approx 66"/167.5cm, or desired length. Bind off.

striped sonata

Want just the thing to help you make a snowball? Look no further than these striped mittens: in addition to being suited for snowball formation, their cute pattern will put a song in your heart! "Striped Sonata" was designed by Charlotte Parry and featured in the Winter '05/'06 issue of *Family Circle Easy Knitting.*

MITTENS SIZED FOR CHILDREN, WOMEN, MEN.

MATERIALS

TLC Essentials by Coats & Clark, 5oz/140g skeins, each approx 326yd/298m (acrylic)

  1 skein each in #2254 persimmon (A) and #2220 butter (B)

  Five size 6 (4mm) dp needles, OR SIZE TO OBTAIN GAUGE

  Safety pin or small stitch holder

FINISHED MEASUREMENTS

  Length from wrist to fingertips 7 (10, 11)" /18 (25.5, 28)cm

  Wrist circumference 5¼ (6½, 7½)"/13.5 (16.5, 19)cm

GAUGE

  20 sts and 28 rows to 4"/10cm over St st using size 6 (4mm) needles.

  TAKE TIME TO CHECK YOUR GAUGE.

NOTE

Work each mitten in alternating 2-row stripes of A and B.

LEFT MITTEN

Cast on 8 (10, 12) sts on first dpn, 8 (10, 12) sts on 2nd dpn 8 (10, 12) sts on 3rd dpn and 8 (10, 12) sts on 4th dpn—32 (40, 48) sts.

Pm to mark beg of rnd and join. Work in k1, p1 rib for 2 (3, 3)"/5 (7.5, 7.5)cm.

Change to St st and work even for 3 rows

Base of thumb

Rnd 1 K12 (16, 20), M1, k2, M1, k rem sts to end—34 (42, 50) sts.

Rnds 2 and 3 Knit.

Rnd 4 K12 (16, 20), M1, k4, M1, k rem sts to end—36 (44, 52) sts.

Rnds 5 and 6 Knit.

Rnd 7 K12 (16, 20), M1, k6, M1, k rem sts to end—38 (46, 54) sts.

Rnds 8 and 9 Knit.

Rnd 10 K12 (16, 20), M1, k8, M1, k rem sts to end—40 (48, 56) sts.

Rnds 11 and 12 Knit.

Rnd 13 K12 (16, 20), M1, k10, M1, k rem sts—42 (50, 58) sts.

For women's and men's sizes only

Rnds 14 and **15** Knit.

Rnd 16 K (16, 20), M1, k12, M1, k rem sts to end—(52, 60) sts.

Rnd 17 Knit.

For men's size only

Rnds 18 and **19** Knit.

Rnd 20 K 20, M1, k14, M1, k rem sts to end—62 sts.

Rnd 21 Knit.

For all sizes

Next rnd K12 (16, 20), place next 12 (14, 16) sts on a holder (either a contrast color strand of yarn or a small stitch holder) for thumb, k to end.

Next rnd K12 (16, 20), cast on 2 sts, k to end of rnd—32 (40, 48) sts. Cont in St st on 32 (40, 48) sts for hand of mitten until piece is 5½ (8½, 9½)"/14 (21.5, 24)cm, or until piece is long enough to cover index fingernail.

Mitten top shaping

Rnd 1 K1, SKP, k10 (14, 18), k2tog, k2, SKP, k10 (14, 18), k2tog, k1—28 (36, 44) sts.

Rnd 2 K1, SKP, k8 (12, 16), k2tog, k2, SKP, k8 (12, 16) sts, k2tog, k1—24 (32, 40) sts.

Rnd 3 K1, SKP, k6 (10, 14), k2tog, k2, SKP, k6 (10, 14), k2tog, k1—20 (28, 36) sts.

Rnd 4 K1, SKP, k4 (8, 12), k2tog, k2, SKP, k4 (8, 12), k2tog, k1—16 (24, 32) sts.

Rnd 5 K1, SKP, k2 (6, 10), k2tog, k2, SKP, k2 (6, 10), k2tog, k1—12 (20, 28) sts.

For women's and men's sizes only

Rnd 6 K1, SKP, k (4, 8), k2tog, k2, SKP, k (4, 8), k2tog, k1—(16, 24) sts.

Rnd 7 K1, SKP, k (2, 6), k2tog, k2, SKP, k (2, 6), k2tog, k1—(12, 20) sts.

For men's size only

Rnd 8 K1, SKP, k4, k2tog, k2, SKP, k4, k2tog, k1—16 sts.

Rnd 9 K1, SKP, k2, k2tog, k2, SKP, k2, k2tog, k1—12 sts.

For all sizes

Last rnd K1, SKP, k2tog, k2, SKP, k2tog, k1—8 sts.

Cut yarn, draw yarn end through rem 8 sts and fasten off.

Thumb

Pick up 5 (6, 7) sts from 12 (14, 16) sts on holder with first dpn, 5 (6, 7) sts with 2nd dpn and 2 sts with 3rd dpn; pick up and knit 2 sts from hand of mitten—14 (16, 18) sts.

Work even in St st until thumb measures 1¼ (2, 2¼)"/3.5 (5, 6)cm, or long enough to cover half of thumbnail.

Next row [K2tog, k1] 4 (5, 6) times, k2 (1, 0)—10 (11, 12) sts.

Next row [K2 tog] 5 (5, 6) times, k0 (1, 0) — 5 (6, 6) sts.

Next row [K2 tog] 2 (3, 3) times, k1 (0, 0)—3 sts.

Cut yarn, draw yarn end through rem 3 sts and fasten off.

RIGHT MITTEN

Work as for left mitten except position base of thumb as follows:

Rnd 1 K18 (22, 26), M1, k2, M1, K rem sts to end—34 (42, 50) sts. Shape remainder of thumb base as for left mitten.

around the block

Despite the name, Granny squares are ageless! Here Sandi Prosser joins them together for a hip, youthful scarf finished with cluster-stitch edging. "Around the Block" first appeared in the Fall '03 issue of *Family Circle Easy Knitting*.

MATERIALS

Soft-Kid by GGH/Muench Yarns, .85oz/25g balls, each approx 150yd/138m (mohair/polyamide/wool)

    5 balls in #71 red

    Size G/6 (4mm) crochet hook OR SIZE TO OBTAIN GAUGE

FINISHED MEASUREMENTS

    10" x 54"/25.5cm x 137cm

GAUGE

    One square to 4"/10cm using size G/6 (4.5mm) crochet hook. TAKE TIME TO CHECK YOUR GAUGE.

STITCH GLOSSARY

Two-Stitch Cluster (2CL)

    [Yo, draw up a lp, yo and draw through 2 lps on hook] twice, yo and draw through all 3 lps on hook.

Three-Stitch Cluster (3CL)

    [Yo, draw up a lp, yo and draw through 2 lps on hook] 3 times, yo and draw through all 4 lps on hook.

SQUARES

(make 26)

Ch 8. Join ch with a sl st forming a ring.

Rnd 1 Ch 3, dc in ring, ch 2, *2CL in ring, ch 2; rep from * around 11 times. Join rnd with a sl st in 3rd ch of ch-3—12 ch-2 sps.

Rnd 2 Sl in first ch-2 sp, ch 3, work 2CL in same ch-2 sp (beg CL made), ch 3, *3CL in next ch-2 sp, ch 3; rep from * 11 times more. Join rnd with a sl st in top of beg CL st.

Rnd 3 Ch 5 (counts as 1 hdc and ch 3) skip first ch-3 sp, in next ch-3 sp, work (3CL, ch 2, 3CL, ch 4, 3CL, ch 2, 3CL), ch 3, *skip next ch-3 sp, hdc in top of next 3CL, ch 3, skip next ch-3 sp, in next ch-3 sp, work (3CL, ch 2, 3CL, ch 4, 3CL, ch 2, 3CL), ch 3; rep from * 3 times. Join rnd with a sl st in 2nd ch of ch-5.

Rnd 4 Ch 1, sc in same ch as joining sl st, *work 3 sc in next ch-3 sp, sc in top of next 3CL, work 2 sc in next ch-2 sp, sc in top of next 3CL, work 5 sc in next ch-4 sp, sc in top of next 3CL, work 2 sc in next ch-2 sp, sc in top of next 3CL, work 3 sc in next ch-3 sp, sc in next hdc; rep from * around 4 times, end last rep omitting sc in next hdc. Join rnd with a sl st in ch-1. Fasten off.

FINISHING

Sew two squares tog to form rows, then sew 13 rows tog to form scarf.

EDGING

From RS, join yarn with a sl st in center st of any corner.

Rnd 1 Ch 1, *work (sc, ch 1, sc) in corner st, sc in each st and seam to next corner center st; rep from * around. Join rnd with a sl st in first sc.

Rnd 2 Sl st in corner ch-1 sp, ch 3 (counts as 1 dc), work (2CL, ch 4, 3CL) in same ch-1 sp, ch 3, skip next 2 sts, 3CL in next st, [*ch 3, sk next 3 sts, 3CL in next st; rep from * to next corner ch-1 sp, work (3CL, ch 4, 3CL) in corner ch-1 sp, ch 3, skip next 2 sts, 3CL in next st] 3 times, end *ch 3, sk next 3 sts, 3CL in next st; rep from * to first corner, ch 3. Join rnd with a sl st in top of 2CL.

Rnd 3 Sl st in corner ch-4 sp, ch 3 (counts as 1 dc), work (2CL, ch 4, 3CL) in same ch-4 sp, [*ch 3, 3CL in next ch-sp; rep from * to next corner ch-4 sp, work (3CL, ch 4, 3CL) in corner ch-4 sp] 3 times, end *ch 3, 3CL in next ch-sp; rep from * to first corner, ch 3. Join rnd with a sl st in top of 2CL.

Rnd 4 Sl st in corner ch-4 sp, work 4 sc in same ch-4 sp, [*sc in top of next 3CL, work 2 sc in next ch-sp; rep from * to next corner ch-4 sp, work 4 sc in ch-4 sp] 3 times, end *sc in top of next 3CL, work 2 sc in next ch-sp; rep from * to first corner, sc in top of 2CL. Join rnd with a sl st in first sc. Fasten off. Lightly block piece to measurements.

cap it off

Greet the great outdoors with these woodsy headwarmers by Irina Poludnenko. Knit from the top down in stockinette stitch with garter stitch ridges, they also feature earflaps that descend into I-cord tassels. "Cap It Off" first appeared in the Winter '03/'04 issue of *Family Circle Easy Knitting*.

MATERIALS

Merino Cablé by S. Charles Collezione/Tahki•Stacy Charles, Inc., 1¾oz/50g balls, each approx 83yd/75m (wool)

Woman's version

    2 balls in #103 dk green (A)

    1 ball in #111 lt green (B)

Man's version

    2 balls in #105 brown (A)

    1 ball each in #101 tan (B), #103 dk green (C) and #111 lt green (D)

Both versions

    One pair size 9 (5.5mm) needles OR SIZE TO OBTAIN GAUGE

    Two size 9 (5.5mm) dpn for I-cord

    Stitch holders and markers

FINISHED MEASUREMENTS

    Head circumference 21½"/54.5cm

GAUGE

    16 sts and 24 rows to 4"/10cm over St st using size 9 (5.5mm) needles.

    TAKE TIME TO CHECK YOUR GAUGE.

Note

Hats are written for one size. To adjust size of head circumference, work fewer or more increases before beginning the stripe pat.

Size

His & Her hats sized for one size fits most.

BOTH VERSIONS

With A, cast on 8 sts for top of hat. P 1 row on WS.

Row 1 (RS) Sl 1, *pm, M1, k1; rep from * 5 times more, p1—14 sts.

Row 2 Purl.

Row 3 Sl 1, *sl marker, M1, k to next marker; rep from * to last st, p1.

Rep rows 2 and 3 (6 sts inc'd every RS row) until there are 86 sts, end with a WS row.

WOMAN'S VERSION

Cont in stripe pat as foll: [With B, k 4 rows. With A, k 1 row, p 1 row] 5 times. With B, k 3 rows.

Next row (WS) Bind off 12 sts, *k until there are 13 sts on RH needle and slip these sts to a holder for earflap*, bind off 36 sts, rep between *'s once, bind off rem 12 sts.

Earflaps

With RS facing and A, k 13 sts from one earflap holder. P 1 row.

Next row Ssk, k to last 2 sts, k2tog. P 1 row. Rep last 2 row until 5 sts rem. Change to dpn and work I-cord as foll: *Next row (RS) K5, do not turn. Slip sts back to beg of row to work next row from RS, bring yarn around from back of work; rep from * until I-cord measures approx 13"/33cm. Bind off.

FINISHING

Sew back seam. Cut strands of A and B each approx 7"/17.5cm and make two tassels. Sew to end of each I-cord.

MAN'S VERSION

Cont in garter st and work in stripe pat as foll: 2 rows each B, A, B, C, B, D, B, A, B, D, B, C, B, A, B. With A, work in St st for 5 rows.

Next row (WS) Bind off 12 sts, *k until there are 13 sts on RH needle and slip these sts to a holder for earflap*, bind off 36 sts, rep between *'s once, bind off rem 12 sts.

Earflaps

With RS facing and A, k 13 sts from one earflap holder. P 1 row. Next row Ssk, k to last 2 sts, k2tog. P 1 row. Rep last 2 row until 5 sts rem. Change to dpn and work I-cord same as woman's version for approx 13"/33cm. Bind off.

FINISHING

Sew back seam.

Bobbles

With B, cast on 3 sts. P 1 row.

Next row K1, M1, k1, M1, k1. P 1 row.

Next row K1, M1, k3, M1, k1—7 sts. P 1 row.

Work in St st for 4 rows.

Next row (RS) K1, ssk, k1, k2tog, k1. P 1 row.

Next row K1, k3tog, k1. P 1 row.

Next row K1, k2tog. Cut yarn and draw through rem 2 sts. Shape piece into a button and sew to top of hat.

Make two more buttons in same way, 1 with C and 1 with D and sew to end of each I-cord.

timeless topper

The enduring beauty of Fair Isle translates into a darling hat for all ages. Designed by Jacqueline Van Dillen, it's capped with a two-tone pompom for good measure. "Timeless Topper" first appeared in the Holiday '02 issue of *Family Circle Easy Knitting.*

MATERIALS

Knitusa by Lane Borgosesia/Trendsetter Yarns, 3½oz/100g balls, each approx 110yds/101m (wool)

> 1 ball #3793 red (A), #95005 white (B)
>
> One pair size 10½ (7mm) needles OR SIZE TO OBTAIN GAUGE

FINISHED MEASUREMENTS

> Head circumference approx 20"/50.5cm

GAUGE

> 13 sts and 15 rows to 4"/10cm over St st and chart pat using size 10½ (7mm) needles.
>
> TAKE TIME TO CHECK YOUR GAUGE.

Size

> Hat in one size.

HAT

With A, cast on 65 sts. Work in k1, p1 rib for 6 rows. Cont in St st and chart pat as foll: **Row 1 (RS)** Work 8-st rep 8 times, work first st of chart once more. Cont as established through row 20. Cut yarn, leaving an end for sewing. Draw end through sts on needle. Pull tog tightly and secure.

FINISHING

Sew back seam. With A, make a 3"/8cm pompom and sew to top of hat.

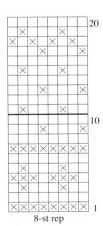

8-st rep

Color Key

☐ Red (A)

☒ White (B)

a need for tweed

Charlotte Parry's mittens prove that it doesn't take much to turn blah mittens into something completely original. A 10-stitch cable perks things up, as does sumptuous multicolored yarn. "A Need for Tweed" first appeared in the Holiday '02 issue of *Family Circle Easy Knitting.*

MATERIALS

Red Heart Tweed by Coats & Clark, 4oz/125g balls, each approx 222yd/204m (acrylic)

    1 ball in #7074 red multi

One pair size 7 (4.5mm) needles OR SIZE TO OBTAIN GAUGE

Cable needle and stitch holders

GAUGE

    20 sts and 26 rows to 4"/10cm over St st using size 7 (4.5mm) needles.

    TAKE TIME TO CHECK YOUR GAUGE.

Size

    Mittens in one size

CABLE PATTERN (OVER 10 STS)

Rows 1 and 3 (RS) P2, k6, p2. **Rows 2, 4 and 6** K2, p6, k2. **Row 5** P2, sl 3 sts to cn and hold to back, k3, k3 from cn, p2. Rep rows 1-6 for cable pat.

RIGHT MITTEN

With size 7 (4.5mm) needles, cast on 40 sts.

Row 1 (RS) K6, work 10 sts cable pat, k24. Cont in St st and cable pat until piece measures 2"/5cm from beg. **Next (inc) row** K1, inc 1, k4, work 10 sts cable pat, k4, inc 1, k2, inc 1, k14, inc 1, k1. Work 1 row even. **Next (inc) row** K1, inc 1, k5, work 10 sts cable pat, k5, inc 1, k2, inc 1, k16, inc 1, k1—48 sts. Work 1 row even. **Next (inc) row** Work 25 sts, [inc 1] twice, k21. Work 3 rows even. **Next (inc) row** Work 26 sts, [inc 1] twice, k22—52 sts. Work even until piece measures 5"/12.5cm from beg. Cut yarn.

Beg thumb

Sl first 22 sts to a holder, join yarn and inc 1, k10, inc 1, sl last 18 sts to a holder. Work these 14 sts in St st for 2"/5cm.

Thumb shaping

Next row (RS) K2tog across. **Next row** P2tog 3 times, p1—4 sts. Draw yarn through rem sts and pull tightly.

Hand

Join yarn and work 22 sts from first holder, pick up and k 2 sts from each side of thumb, work across 18 sts of 2nd holder—44 sts. Cont in pat until piece measures 8"/20.5cm from beg.

Top shaping

Next row (RS) K1, SKP, work 19 sts, k2tog, SKP, k15, k2tog, k1—40 sts. Work 1 row even. **Next row** K1, SKP, work 17 sts, k2tog, SKP, k13, k2tog, k1—36 sts. Work 1 row even. **Next row** K1, SKP, work 15 sts, k2tog, SKP, k11, k2tog, k1—32 sts. Work 1 row even. **Next row** K1, SKP, k2, p2, [k2tog] 3 times, p2, k1, k2tog, SKP, k9, k2tog, k1—25 sts. Work 1 row even. Bind off.

LEFT MITTEN

Work as for right mitten, reversing shaping and pat as foll: K24, work 10 sts cable pat, k6.

FINISHING

Block pieces. Sew thumb. Sew top of mitten and side seam.

match made in heaven

Hit the slopes in complementary accessories designed by Norah Gaughan. Seed stitch makes her duo unique yet understated, while deep ribbing makes his set a hearty hit. "Match Made in Heaven" first appeared in the Winter '03/'04 issue of *Family Circle Easy Knitting*.

MATERIALS

Blizzard by Reynolds/JCA, 1¾oz/50g balls, each approx 66yd/60m (alpaca/acrylic)

Woman's version

   4 balls in #612 lt blue (scarf)

   2 balls in #612 lt blue (hat)

Man's version

   4 balls in #683 dk blue (scarf)

   2 balls in #683 dk blue (hat)

Both versions

   One pair size 13 (9mm) needles OR SIZE TO OBTAIN GAUGE

FINISHED MEASUREMENTS

   Head circumference will stretch to approx 20-21"/50.5-53cm

   Woman's scarf approx 8" x 60"/20.5cm x 152cm

   Man's scarf approx 8" x 72"/20.5cm x 183cm

GAUGES

10 sts and 16 rows to 4"/10cm over seed st using size 13 (9mm) needles.

12 sts and 12 rows to 4"/10cm over rib pat or k1, p1 rib (slightly stretched) using size 13 (9mm) needles.

TAKE TIME TO CHECK YOUR GAUGES.

Note

Hats are written for one size. Due to the nature of the rib patterns, the head will stretch to fit most sizes. If desired, you can adjust the length before the top, decreasing to make it longer or shorter.

SEED STITCH

Row 1 (RS) *K1, p1; rep from * to end.

Row 2 K the purl sts and p the knit sts.

Rep row 2 for seed st.

WOMAN'S SCARF

Cast on 24 sts. Work in seed st for 6"/15.5cm, end with a WS row.

Eyelet row (RS) K1, *yo, k2tog; rep from * to last st, p1. Work in k1, p1 rib until piece measures 54"/137cm from beg. Rep eyelet row, then work in seed st for 6"/15.5cm. Bind off.

WOMAN'S HAT

Cast on 44 sts. Work in seed st for 3"/7.5cm, inc 8 sts evenly across last WS row—52 sts. Work eyelet row as on scarf. Work in k1, p1 rib until piece measures 7"/17.5cm from beg, or desired depth. **Next row (RS)** K1, *k2tog; rep from *, end k1—27 sts. **Next row** P1, p2tog across. Cut yarn and draw through rem 14 sts on needle. Sew back seam.

RIB PAT FOR MAN'S SCARF

(multiple of 10 sts plus 4)

Row 1 *[P1, k1] twice, p3, k3; rep from *, end [p1, k1] twice.

Row 2 K the knit sts and p the purl sts.

Rep row 2 for rib pat.

MAN'S SCARF

Cast on 24 sts. Work in rib pat for 72"/183cm, or desired length. Bind off in pat.

RIB PAT FOR MAN'S SCARF

(multiple of 10 sts plus 2)

Row 1 K1, *[p1, k1] twice, p3, k3; rep from *, end k1.

Row 2 K the knit sts and p the purl sts.

Rep row 2 for rib pat.

MAN'S HAT

Cast on 42 sts. Work in rib pat for 12"/30.5cm or desired depth.

Next row (RS) K2tog across—21 sts.

Cut yarn and draw through rem sts on needle. Sew back seam, reversing seam at 4"/10cm at lower edge for turn back.

the original hoodie

Long before zip-up sweatshirts became de rigueur, the scarf and hood hybrid was a practical way to keep your ears and neck fashionably toasty. Cleckheaton Design Studio brings the look up to the present, adding wide ribs for a comfy, though not snug, fit. "The Original Hoodie" first appeared in the Winter '99/'00 issue of *Family Circle Easy Knitting*.

MATERIALS

Colorwaves, 3oz/85g balls, each approx 98yd/89m
(wool/ acrylic/mohair/viscose)

   6 balls in #108 burgundy

   One pair size 9 (5.5mm) needles OR SIZE TO OBTAIN GAUGE

FINISHED MEASUREMENTS

   Head circumference 22"/56cm

   Length 75"/190cm

GAUGE

   16 sts and 20 rows to 4"/10cm over k9, p9 rib using 9 (5.5mm) needles.

   TAKE TIME TO CHECK YOUR GAUGE.

Size

   Shown in one size.

HOOD AND SCARF

(worked in one piece)

Cast on 45 sts, and work as foll:

Row 1 *K9, p9; rep from * to last 9 sts, k9. **Row 2** K the knit sts and p the purl sts. Rep last row for k9, p9 rib until piece measures 28"/71cm from beg, end with a WS row. Mark end of last row for neck edge. Cont in pat until piece measures 35"/89cm from beg, end with a WS row.

Beg Shaping for Back of Head

Cont in pat, dec one st at beg of next row, then every other row until 39 sts rem. Work 1 row even. Cont in pat, inc one st at beg of next row then every other row until there are 45 sts. Work even until piece measures 18"/46cm from marker, end with a WS row. Mark end of last row for neck edge. Cont until piece measures 28"/71cm from 2nd marker, with a WS row. Bind off loosely in rib.

FINISHING

Sew back of head between markers.

helmet head

You'll never have to worry about frostbite with this homage to the military uniform of yore. Complete with earflaps and a quick whip-stitched edge, the hat is totally up-to-the-minute. The duo is knit in garter stitch, revealing the subdued shades hidden in the yarn's variegated fibers. "Helmet Head" first appeared in the Winter '99/'00 issue of *Family Circle Easy Knitting*.

MATERIALS

Cleckheaton Snowflake 8 Ply by Plymouth Yarn, 1¾oz/50g ball, each approx 94yd/85m (wool/polyamide/polyester)

Mittens

   2 balls in #2174 red multi (MC)

   Small amounts of Country 8 Ply in #0006 black (CC)

   One pair size 6 (4mm) needles OR SIZE TO OBTAIN GAUGE

Hat

   2 balls in #2174 red multi (MC)

   Small amounts of Country 8 Ply in #0006 black (CC)

   Size 6 (4mm) circular needle, 16"/40cm long OR SIZE TO OBTAIN GAUGE

   One set size 6 (4mm) dpn

   Stitch holders

   Tapestry needle for embroidery

FINISHED MEASUREMENTS

   Wrist 7½"/19cm

   Head circumference 22"/56cm

GAUGE

   21 sts and 44 rows to 4"/10cm over garter st.
   TAKE TIME TO CHECK YOUR GAUGE.

Size

   Shown in one size

MITTENS

RIGHT MITTEN

With MC, cast on 40 sts. Work in garter st for 16 rows.

Hand shaping

Row 1 (RS) K21, k in front and back of next st (inc 1), k1, inc 1, k16—42 sts. K 3 rows.

Row 5 K21, inc 1, k3, inc 1, k16—44 sts. K 3 rows.

Row 9 K21, inc 1, k5, inc 1, k16—46 sts.

Cont inc in this way to inc 2 sts every 4th row until there are 50 sts. K 3 rows.

Thumb shaping

Next row (RS) K32, turn.

Next row K12, turn, cast on 3 sts—15 sts.

K 18 rows on these 15 sts.

Top shaping

Row 1 *K1, k2tog; rep from * to end—10 sts.

Row 2 Knit.

Row 3 *K2tog; rep from * to end—5 sts.

Break yarn, thread through rem sts and fasten off securely.

With RS facing, join yarn to rem sts, pick up and k 3 sts from cast on sts at base of thumb, then k to end—41 sts. K 29 rows, inc 1 st in center of last row—42 sts.

Top shaping

Row 1 (RS) [K1, SKP, k15, k2tog, k1] twice—38 sts.

Row 2 and all WS rows Knit.

Row 3 [K1, SKP k13, k2tog, k1] twice—34 sts.

Cont in this way to dec 4 sts every RS row until 14 sts rem.

LEFT MITTEN

Work as for right mitten, reversing hand shaping as foll:

Hand shaping

Row 1 K16, inc 1, k1, inc 1, k21—42 sts. K 3 rows.

Row 5 K16, inc 1, k3, inc 1, k21—44 sts. K 3 rows.

Cont inc in this way to inc 2 sts every 4th row until there are 50 sts. K 3 rows.

Thumb shaping

Next row K32, turn, cast on 3 sts.

Next row K15, turn.

Complete to correspond to right mitten.

FINISHING

Sew thumb and hand seams. With CC, embroider blanket st around edge of cuffs.

HAT

EAR FLAPS (make 2)

With MC, cast on 9 sts. Work 2 rows garter st. Cont in garter st, inc 1 st each side of next row then every other row once more, then in every 4th row until there are 19 sts. Work even until piece measures 3"/8cm from beg, end with a WS row. Next row Inc 1 st each side of next row then every other row until there are 25 sts. K 1 row. Place sts on a holder.

HAT

(**Note** Change to dpn when there are too few sts to fit on circular needle.)

With circular needle and MC, cast on 13 sts, knit across sts from first earflap holder, cast on 36 sts, knit across sts from 2nd earflap holder, cast on 13 sts—112 sts. Join, taking care not to twist sts on needle.

Work in garter st (p 1 rnd, k 1 rnd) until piece measures 4"/10cm from beg, end with a p rnd.

Crown shaping

Rnd 1 *K2tog, k12; rep from * to end—104 sts.

Rnd 2 and every other rnd Purl.

Rnd 3 *K2tog, k11; rep from * to end—96 sts.

Rnd 5 *K2tog, K10; rep from * to end—88 sts.

Cont in this way to dec 8 sts every other rnd until 16 sts rem.

Next rnd K2tog around—8 sts.

Top point

Rnd 1 Purl. Rnd 2 Knit. Rep last 2 rnds 3 times. Break yarn, thread through rem sts, draw up and fasten off securely.

FINISHING

With CC embroider blanket st around ear flaps and base of hat.

Tassels

With CC, wind yarn 8 times around a piece of cardboard 4"/10cm long to make tassel. With CC make 2 twisted cords approx 7"/18cm long, attach tassel to end of twisted cord, stitch to center of each earflap.

the long way

Sandi Prosser turns the crocheted scarf on its head, working strips of color lengthwise in this offbeat design. Go for broke with some funky fringe (not shown) for the full effect. "The Long Way" first appeared in the Fall '03 issue of *Family Circle Easy Knitting*.

FINISHED MEASUREMENTS

8¼" x 90"/21cm x 228.5cm (without fringe)

GAUGE

10 sts and 12 rows to 4"/10cm over sc using size K/10 1/2 (6.5mm) crochet hook.

TAKE TIME TO CHECK YOUR GAUGE.

Note

When changing color, draw new color through 2 lps on hook to complete last sc, then ch 1 and turn.

STRIPE PATTERN

Working in sc, work 1 row B, 2 rows C, 1 row D, 2 rows each in E and F, 1 row G, 2 rows H, 1 row G, 2 rows each in F and E, 1 row D, 2 rows each in C and B and 1 row A.

SCARF

Beg at side edge, with A, ch 226.

Row 1 Sc in 2nd ch from hook and in each ch across—225 sts. Join B, ch 1, turn.

Row 2 Sc in each st across. Ch 1, turn. Rep row 2 for pat st and work even in stripe pat—24 rows completed. Fasten off.

FINISHING

Fringe

For each fringe, cut one strand 20"/51cm long. Use crochet hook to pull through and knot fringe. Using color that corresponds to row color, knot one fringe in each row along each end.

must-have mittens

Chunky single cables grace the top of these classy mittens from designer Veronica Manno. Knit in cashmere—one of the most luxurious fibers in the world—this pair will be the silkiest and softest you ever own! "Must-Have Mittens" first appeared in the Holiday '02 issue of *Family Circle Easy Knitting*.

MATERIALS

Sinful by Classic Elite Yarns, 1¾oz/50g each approx 65yds/60m (cashmere)

   2 balls in #92028 red

   One pair size 10 (6mm) needles OR SIZE TO OBTAIN GAUGE

   Cable needle

   Stitch holder

GAUGE

   14 sts and 20 rows to 4"/10cm over St st using size 10 (6mm) needles.

   TAKE TIME TO CHECK YOUR GAUGE.

Size

   Mittens in one size.

CABLE PATTERN

(over 8 sts)

Rows 1, 3 and 7 (RS) P1, k6, p1.

Rows 2, 4, 6 and 8 K1, p6, k1.

Row 5 P1, sl 3 sts to cn and hold to front, k3, k3 from cn, p1.

Rep rows 1-8 for cable pat.

RIGHT MITTEN

Cast on 26 sts. Work in k2, p2 rib for 3"/7.5cm.

Beg cable pat

Next row (RS) Work 3 sts in st st, 8 sts in cable pat, work in St st to end. Cont as established for 7 rows more.

Thumb gusset

Next (inc) row Work 12 sts, M1, k1, M1, work to end. Work 1 row even.

Next (inc) row Work 12 sts, M1, k3, M1, work to end. Work 1 row even.

Next (inc) row Work 12 sts, M1, k5, M1, work to end. Work 1 row even—32 sts.

HAND

Next row (RS) Work 12 sts, place next 7 sts on a holder for thumb, cast on 1 st, work to end—26 sts. Cont in St st until piece measures 4"/10 from thumb sts or 2"/5cm less than desired length.

Top shaping

Next row (RS) SKP, k9, k2tog, SKP, k9, k2tog—22 sts. P 1 row. **Next row** SKP, k7, k2tog, SKP, k7, k2tog—18 sts. P 1 row. Cont in this way to dec 4 sts every other row 3 times more—6 sts. Bind off.

Thumb

Next row (RS) Sl sts from holder to needle, pick up 1 st at inside of gusset—8 sts. Work in St st for 1¾"/4.5cm, or desired length. **Next row (RS)** *K2tog; rep from * around. Cut yarn and draw through rem 4 sts. Pull tog tightly and secure.

FINISHING

Sew side and thumb seams.

LEFT MITTEN

Work as for right mitten, reversing all shaping and pat placement as foll: K15, work 8 sts cable pat, k3. Reverse thumb placement as foll: **Next row (RS)** K13, M1, k1, M1, work to end.

mixed media

Beginners will love Nicky Epstein's festive multi-yarn scarves, created in bands of various weights and fibers. Try stockinette or garter stitch, or use them together for something truly original. "Mixed Media" first appeared in the Holiday '04 issue of *Family Circle Easy Knitting*.

MATERIALS

Small amounts of coordinating red yarns in various weights and qualities

One pair size 10 (6mm) needles OR SIZE TO OBTAIN GAUGE

FINISHED MEASUREMENTS

Girl's scarf

Approx 4"/10cm wide by 50"/127cm long

Woman's scarf

Approx 8"/20.5cm wide by 86"/218cm long

Notes

1 These scarves were made using small amounts of red yarns from various sources in different weights and qualities.

2 Only one needle size was used, creating different gauges for the different yarns.

3 Yarns and colors are changed randomly.

SCARF

Cast on 10 sts (for girl's), 32 sts (for woman's). Work in garter st (for girl's), St st (for woman's), changing yarns and colors as desired, for 50"/127cm (for girl's), 86"/218cm (for woman's), or desired length. Bind off.

put up your mitts

No boring mittens for you: strut your stuff in flashy hues of red, gold, and green, with ecru ribbing. Designed by Charlotte Parry, "Put Up Your Mitts" first appeared in the Fall '05 issue of *Family Circle Easy Knitting.*

MITTENS SIZED FOR CHILDREN, WOMEN, MEN.

MATERIALS

TLC Essentials by Coats & Clark, 5oz/140g skeins, each approx 326yd/298m (acrylic)

- 1 skein each in #2313 aran (A), #2673 medium thyme (B), #2220 butter (C) and #2254 persimmon (D)
- Five size 6 (4mm) dp needles, OR SIZE TO OBTAIN GAUGE
- Safety pin or small stitch holder

FINISHED MEASUREMENTS

Length from wrist to fingertips 7 (10, 11)"/18 (25.5, 28)cm

Wrist circumference 5¼ (6½, 7½)"/13.5 (16.5,19)cm

GAUGE

20 sts and 28 rows to 4"/10cm over St st using size 6 (4mm) needles. TAKE TIME TO CHECK YOUR GAUGE.

MITTENS

Work as for striped mittens, page 76. Work rib with A; 28 rnds of hand and up to base of thumb with B; remainder of hand with C and top of thumb with D.

two for the road

Reversible cables and fringed edges make an ordinary scarf extraordinary! Designer Michelle Woodford uses ever-so-current green for her and a variegated brown for him. "Two for the Road" first appeared in the Winter '03/'04 issue of *Family Circle Easy Knitting.*

MATERIALS

Fiamma by DiVé/Cascade Yarns Inc, 1¾oz/50g balls, each approx 55yds/50m (wool)

- 7 balls in #27385 lt green (woman's) or #14946 brown (man's)
- One pair size 11 (8mm) needles OR SIZE TO OBTAIN GAUGE
- Cable needle
- Stitch markers

FINISHED MEASUREMENTS

Approx 8" x 68"/20.5cm x 172.5cm

GAUGE

12 sts and 15 rows to 4"/10cm over St st using size 11 (8mm) needles.

TAKE TIME TO CHECK YOUR GAUGE.

STITCH GLOSSARY

6–st RC

Sl 3 sts to cn and hold to back of work, k3, k3 from cn.

SCARF

Cast on 30 sts.

Beg pat

Row 1 (WS) [P1, k1] 3 times, p6, k6, p6, [k1, p1] 3 times.

Row 2 K the knit sts and p the purl sts.

Rep rows 1 and 2 twice more. Rep row 1 once.

Row 8 (RS cable row, mark this row with a st marker to keep track of cable rows) [K1, p1], 6-st RC, p6, 6-st RC, [p1, k1] 3 times.

Row 9 (WS cable row) [P1, k1] 3 times, p6, 6-st RC, p6, [k1, p1] 3 times.

Row 10 Rep row 1.

Rep rows 1-10 for pat until piece measures approx 68"/172.5cm from beg, end with a pat row 5. Bind off in pat.

FINISHING

Block lightly to measurements, being careful not to press cables flat.

Fringe

Cut 32"/81cm lengths of yarn. Fold 1 strand in half (for double fringe) and attach 30 double fringe to each end of scarf. Trim fringe.

the switch-hitter

Who says you can't make all of the people happy all of the time? Carla Scott certainly succeeds with this I-cord and stockinette stitch concoction: work back and forth, or knit in the round for a seamless finish. How's that for options? "The Switch Hitter" first appeared in the Fall '04 issue of *Family Circle Easy Knitting.*

MATERIALS

Skye Tweed by Classic Elite Yarns, 1¾oz/50g balls, each approx 112yd/103m (wool)

- 1 ball each in #1235 green (A), #1258 red (B), #1285 orange (C) and #1208 blue (D)
- Size 9 (4.5mm) needles, one pair (for working back and forth) OR circular 16"/40cm long (for working in the round) OR SIZE TO OBTAIN GAUGE
- One set (4) size 9 (4.5mm) dpn

FINISHED MEASUREMENTS

Head circumference 21"/53.5cm

GAUGE

17 sts and 24 rows (rnds) to 4"/10cm over St st using size 9 (4.5mm) needles.

TAKE TIME TO CHECK YOUR GAUGE.

Size

Hat in one size

STRIPE PATTERN

*4 rows A, 1 row D, 4 rows B, 1 row D, 4 rows C, 1 row D; rep from * (15 rows) for stripe pat.

HAT

With straight needles (or circular needle) and A, cast on 90 sts. (If working in the round, join taking care not to twist sts on needle. Place marker for end of rnd and center back, and sl marker every rnd. Change to dpn when there are too few sts for circular needle.) Work in St st and stripe pat for 3½"/9cm.

TOP SHAPING

Next row (RS) K4, k2tog, [k8, k2tog] 8 times, k4. Work 1 row even.

Next row K4, k2tog, [k7, k2tog] 8 times, k3. Work 1 row even.

Next row K3, k2tog, [k6, k2tog] 8 times, k3. Work 1 row even.

Next row K3, k2tog, [k5, k2tog] 8 times, k2. Work 1 row even.

Next row K2, k2tog, [k4, k2tog] 8 times, k2. Work 1 row even.

Next row K2, k2tog, [k3, k2tog] 8 times, k1. Work 1 row even.

Next row K1, k2tog, [k2, k2tog] 8 times, k1. Work 1 row even.

Next row K1, k2tog, [k1, k2tog] 8 times. Work 1 row even.

Next row [K2tog] 9 times.

Last row [P2tog] 3 times, p3tog. Cut yarn and draw through rem 4 sts. Pull tog tightly and secure.

EARFLAPS

Count 11 sts from one side edge along cast-on edge. With RS facing and B, beg in the 12th st, pick up and k18 sts along cast-on edge. Work back and forth in St st for 5 rows. **Dec row (RS)** K1, SKP, k to last 3 sts, k2tog, k1. Work 3 rows even. Rep last 4 rows until there are 12 sts. Then rep dec row every other row until 4 sts rem. Change to dpn and work I-cord as foll:

*Next row (RS) K4, do not turn work. Slide sts to beg of row to work next row from RS; rep from * until I-cord measures 6"/15.5cm. Bind off. Rep earflap at 11 sts from other edge.

FINISHING

Sew back seam if necessary.

call it the blues

Sandi Prosser's precious trio is crocheted in a mohair blend for a fuzzy, soft-focus appeal. The seamless hat is a novice's dream, while the trendy (and optional) flowers are worked and attached separately. "Call It the Blues" first appeared in the Holiday '04 issue of *Family Circle Easy Knitting*.

MATERIALS

Kid et Soie by Naturally/S. R. Kertzer, 1¾oz/50g balls, each approx 93yd/85m (mohair/silk/wool)

    9 balls in #302 blue

    Crochet hooks sizes H/8 and I/9 (5 and 5.5mm) OR SIZE TO OBTAIN GAUGE

    Small safety pin

FINISHED MEASUREMENTS

Hat

    Head circumference 20½ (22)"/52 (56)cm

Scarf

    Approx 6½" x 60"/16.5 x 152.5cm

GAUGE

    13 sts and 16 rows to 4"/10cm over sc using larger crochet hook.

    TAKE TIME TO CHECK YOUR GAUGE.

Sizes

    Hat is sized for Small/Medium (Large/X-Large). Scarf and mittens are one size.

STITCH GLOSSARY

dc2tog

[Yo. Insert hook into next st and draw up a lp. Yo and draw through 2 lps] twice, yo and draw through all 3 lps on hook.

sc2tog

[Insert hook into next st and draw up a lp] twice, yo and draw through all 3 lps on hook.

HAT

With larger hook, ch 4. Join ch with a sl st forming a ring.

Rnd 1 Ch 1, work 9 sc in ring. Join this and all rnds with a sl st in first st.

Rnd 2 Ch 1, work 2 sc in same st as joining, work 2 sc in each st around—18 sts. Join.

Rnd 3 Ch 1, sc in same st as joining, sc in next st, *work 2 sc in next st, sc in next 2 sts; rep from * around—24 sts. Join.

Rnd 4 Ch 1, sc in same st as joining, sc in next 2 sts, *work 2 sc in next st, sc in next 3 sts; rep from * around to last st, work 2 sc in last st—30 sts. Join.

Rnd 5 Ch 1, sc in same st as joining, sc in next 3 sts, *work 2 sc in next st, sc in next 4 sts; rep from * around to last st, work 2 sc in last st—36 sts. Join.

Rnd 6 Ch 1, sc in same st as joining, sc in next 4 sts, *work 2 sc in next st, sc in next 5 sts; rep from * around to last st, work 2 sc in last st—42 sts. Join.

Rnd 7 Ch 1, sc in same st as joining, sc in next 5 sts, *work 2 sc in next st, sc in next 6 sts; rep from * around to last st, work 2 sc in last st—48 sts. Join.

Rnd 8 Ch 1, sc in same st as joining, sc in each st around. Join.

Rnd 9 Ch 1, sc in same st as joining, sc in next 6 sts, *work 2 sc in next st, sc in next 7 sts; rep from * around to last st, work 2 sc in last st—54 sts. Join.

Rnd 10 Rep rnd 8.

Rnd 11 Ch 1, sc in same st as joining, sc in next 7 sts, *work 2 sc in next st, sc in next 8 sts; rep from * around to last st, work 2 sc in last st—60 sts. Join.

Rnd 12 Rep rnd 8.

Rnd 13 Ch 1, sc in same st as joining, sc in next 8 sts, *work 2 sc in next st, sc in next 9 sts; rep from * around to last st, work 2 sc in last st—66 sts. Join.

Rnd 14 Rep rnd 8.

For size Small/Medium only

Rep rnd 14 for 12 times more.

For size Large/X-Large only

Rnd 15 Ch 1, sc in same st as joining, sc in next 9 sts, *work 2 sc in next st, sc in next 10 sts; rep from * around to last st, work 2 sc in last st—72 sts. Join. Rep rnd 14 for 15 times more.

For both sizes

Last rnd Ch 1, working from left to right, sc in each st around. Join rnd with a sl st in first st. Fasten off.

FLOWERS

(make 3)

With larger hook, ch 4. Join ch with a sl st forming a ring. Rnd 1 Ch 1, work 15 sc in ring. Join rnd with a sl st in first st.

Rnd 2 [Ch 3, dc2tog, ch 3, sl st in next st] 5 times—5 petals made. Fasten off, leaving a long tail for sewing. Sew on flowers as shown.

SCARF

With larger hook, ch 22.

Row 1 Sc in 2nd ch from hook and in each ch across—21 sts. Ch 1, turn.

Row 2 Sc in each st across. Ch 1, turn. Rep row 2 until piece measures 60"/152.5cm from beg. Fasten off.

FLOWERS

(make 10)

Work as for hat. Sew five flowers on each end of scarf as shown.

RIGHT MITTEN

Cuff

With smaller hook, ch 11.

Row 1 Sc in 2nd ch from hook and in each ch across—10 sts. Ch 1, turn.

Row 2 Working in back lps only, sc in each st across. Ch 1, turn.

Rep row 2 until piece measures, when slightly stretched, 7"/18cm from beg. Change to larger hook. Ch 1, turn to long side edge of cuff.

Next row (RS) Work 27 sc evenly spaced along edge of cuff. Ch 1, turn.

Cont in sc for 5 more rows. Ch 1, turn.

Thumb shaping

Row 1 Sc in first 15 sts, work 2 sc in next st, sc in next st, work 2 sc in next st, sc in last 9 sts—29 sts. Ch 1, turn.

Row 2 Sc in first 9 sts, work 2 sc in next st, sc in next 3 sts, work 2 sc in next st, sc in last 15 sts—31 sts. Ch 1, turn.

Row 3 Sc in first 15 sts, work 2 sc in next st, sc in next 5 sts, work 2 sc in next st, sc in last 9 sts—33 sts. Ch 1, turn.

Row 4 Sc in first 9 sts, work 2 sc in next st, sc in next 7 sts, work 2 sc in next st, sc in last 15 sts—35 sts. Ch 1, turn.

Row 5 Sc in first 15 sts, work 2 sc in next st, sc in next 9 sts, work 2 sc in next st, sc in last 9 sts—37 sts. Ch 1, turn.

Hand

Next row Sc in first 10 sts, ch 1, skip next 11 sts, sc in last 16 sts. Ch 1, turn. **Next row** Sc in each st and ch-1 sp across—27 sts. Place safety pin marker in bottom of sc in ch-1 sp for thumb. Ch 1, turn. Cont in sc until piece measures 6½"/16.5cm above cuff, end with a WS row. Ch 1, turn.

Top shaping

Row 1 (RS) Sc2tog, sc in next 9 sts, sc2tog, sc in next st, sc2tog, sc in next 9 sts, sc2tog—23 sts. Ch 1, turn.

Row 2 Sc in each st across. Ch 1, turn.

Row 3 Sc2tog, sc in next 7 sts, sc2tog, sc in next st, sc2tog, sc in next 7 sts, sc2tog—19 sts. Ch 1, turn.

Row 4 Rep row 2.

Row 5 Sc2tog, sc in next 5 sts, sc2tog, sc in next st, sc2tog, sc in next 5 sts, sc2tog—15 sts. Ch 1, turn.

Fasten off. Sew top and side seam.

Thumb

With larger hook, join yarn with as sl st in bottom of marked st.

Rnd 1 Ch 1, sc in same sp as joining, work 11 sc evenly spaced around opening—12 sts. Join this and all rnds with a sl st in first sc.

Rnd 2 Ch 1, sc in same sp as joining, sc in each st around. Join. Rep rnd 2 until thumb measures 2½"/6cm.

Last rnd Ch 1, [sc2tog] 6 times—6 sts. Fasten off, leaving a long tail. Thread tail into tapestry needle and weave through sts. Pull tight to gather, fasten off securely.

LEFT MITTEN

Work cuff as for right mitten.

Thumb shaping

Row 1 Sc in first 9 sts, work 2 sc in next st, sc in next st, work 2 sc in next st, sc in last 15 sts—29 sts. Ch 1, turn.

Row 2 Sc in first 15 sts, work 2 sc in next st, sc in next 3 sts, work 2 sc in next st, sc in last 9 sts—31 sts. Ch 1, turn.

Row 3 Sc in first 9 sts, work 2 sc in next st, sc in next 5 sts, work 2 sc in next st, sc in last 15 sts—33 sts. Ch 1, turn.

Row 4 Sc in first 15 sts, work 2 sc in next st, sc in next 7 sts, work 2 sc in next st, sc in last 9 sts—35 sts. Ch 1, turn.

Row 5 Sc in first 9 sts, work 2 sc in next st, sc in next 9 sts, work 2 sc in next st, sc in last 15 sts—37 sts. Ch 1, turn.

Hand

Next row Sc in first 16 sts, ch 1, sk next 11 sts, sc in last 10 sts. Ch 1, turn.

Next row Sc in each st and ch-1 sp across—27 sts. Place safety pin marker in bottom of sc in ch-1 sp for thumb. Ch 1, turn. Cont to work as for right mitten.

shell game

Gussy up the typical scarf and hat with a sheer crocheted shell pattern for a pair of accessories that can go for three seasons. Braided fringe makes the muffler even more marvelous. "Shell Game" first appeared in the Fall '04 issue of *Family Circle Easy Knitting*.

MATERIALS

Pleasure by Berroco, Inc., 1¾oz/50g balls, each approx 130yd/120m (angora/wool/nylon)

  3 balls in #8618 brown (A)

  1 ball each in #8650 black (B), #8617 green (C), #8631 blue (D), #8654 wine (E) and #8624 purple (F)

  Sizes I/9 (5.5mm) and J/10 (6mm) crochet hooks OR SIZE TO OBTAIN GAUGE

FINISHED MEASUREMENTS

Hat

  Head circumference 19"/48cm

  Depth 7½"/19cm

Scarf

  7½"/19cm wide and 66"/167.5cm long

GAUGE

  16 sc and 14 rows to 4"/10cm over sc pat using larger crochet hook.

  TAKE TIME TO CHECK YOUR GAUGE.

Size

  Hat and scarf sized for one size.

HAT

Beg at top edge with larger hook and A, ch 4, join with sl st to first ch to form ring.

Rnd 1 With A, work 6 sc in ring, join with sl st to first sc, ch 1.

Rnd 2 With A, work 2 sc in each sc around—12 sc. Ch 1.

Rnd 3 With A, work 1 sc in first sc, *2 sc in next sc, 1 sc in next sc; rep from *, end 2 sc in last sc—18 sc. Draw E through last 2 loops, ch 1.

Rnd 4 With E, work 1 sc in first sc, *2 sc in next sc, 1 sc in each of next 2 sc; rep from *, end sc in last sc—24 sc. Draw F through last 2 loops, ch 1.

Rnd 5 With F, work 1 sc in each of first 2 sc, *2 sc in next sc, 1 sc in each of next 3 sc; rep from *, end 1 sc in last sc—30 sc. Draw through last 2 loops on hook—ch 1.

Rnd 6 With A, working through back loops, sc in each sc around. Draw B through last 2 loops, ch 1.

Rnd 7 With B, work 1 sc in first sc, *2 sc in next sc, 1 sc in each of next 4 sc; rep from *, end sc in last 3 sc—36 sc. Draw C through last 2 loops, ch 1.

Rnd 8 With C, working in back loops, 1 sc in first sc, *2 sc in next sc, 1 sc in each of next 5 sc; rep from *, end sc in last 4 sc—42 sc. Draw B through last 2 loops, ch 1.

Rnd 9 With D, 1 sc in each of first 2 sc, *2 sc in next sc, 1 sc in each of next 6 sc; rep from *, end sc in last 4 sc—48 sc. Draw C through last 2 loops, ch 1.

Rnd 10 With C, 1 sc in first sc, *2 sc in next sc, 1 sc in each of next 7 sc; rep from *, end 1 sc in last 6 sc—54 sc. Draw B through last 2 loops, ch 1.

Rnd 11 With B, 1 sc in first 2 sc, *2 sc in next sc, 1 sc in each of next 8 sc; rep from *, end 1 sc in last 6 sc—60 sc. Draw A through last 2 loops, ch 1.

Rnd 12 With A, working through back loops, *2 sc in next sc, 1 sc in each of next 5 sc; rep from * around—70 sc. Draw F through last 2 loops, ch 1.

Rnd 13 With F, work even in sc. Draw E through last 2 loops, ch 1.

Rnd 14 With E, working through back loops, work even in sc. Draw A through last 2 loops, ch 1.

Rnds 15 and 16 Work even with A. On rnd 16, draw B through last 2 loops, ch 1.

Rnd 17 With B, work even in sc. Draw C through last 2 loops. Ch 1.

Rnd 18 With C, working through back loops, work even in sc. Draw D through last 2 loops. Change to smaller hook.

Rnd 19 With D, ch 6, *skip 4 sc, work (1 dc, ch 2 and 1 dc) in next sc, ch 3; rep from *, end 1 dc in same sc as joining, ch 2, join to 3rd ch of ch-6.

Rnd 20 With D, ch 4 (counts as 1 tr), *skip ch-3 sp, work 5 tr in next ch-2 sp; rep from *, end 4 tr in last ch-2 sp, join with sl st to top of ch-4.

Rnd 21 With D, ch 5 (counts as 1 dc and ch 2), skip first 2 tr, into next tr work (1 dc, ch 2 and 1 dc), *ch 3, skip 4 tr, into next tr work (1 dc, ch 2 and 1 dc); rep from *, end ch 3, join with sl st to 3rd ch of ch-5.

Rnd 22 Rep rnd 20. Draw C through last 2 loops, ch 1.

Rnd 23 With C, work even in sc around—70 sc. Draw through last 2 loops, ch 1.

Rnd 24 With B, sc in back loops. Draw A through last 2 loops, ch 1.

Rnd 25 With A, sc in back loops, ch 1.

Rnd 26 With A, sl st through back loops. Fasten off.

SCARF

Beg above lace edge, with larger hook and C, ch 28.

Row 1 (RS) With C, sc in 2nd ch from hook and in each ch to end—27 sc. Cut C.

Row 2 (RS) Join B to work from RS, ch 1, and work even in sc with B. Cut B.

Row 3 (RS) Join A to work from RS, ch 1 and sc in back loops, ch 1, turn.

Row 4 With A, work even in sc. Work even in sc from RS as foll:

Rows 5–15 Work 1 row with E, 1 row with F, 1 row through back loops with A, 1 row with B, 1 row through back loops with C, 1 row with D, 1 row with C, 1 row with B, 1 row through back loops with A, 1 row with F, 1 row through back loops with E.

Row 16 (RS) With A, ch 2 and working through back loops, work in hdc, inc 1 st each side of row for 29 hdc. Ch 2, turn.

Row 17 (WS) With A, work hdc through front loops. Ch 2, turn.

Rep rows 16 and 17 (omitting inc on row 16) for 46"/117cm above stripe border, dec 1 st each side of last WS row—27 hdc. Then work other stripe border in reverse, that is rows 15-1 only work back loop sc on the foll rows instead: rows 14, 13, 11, 12, 7, 5 and 1.

LACE EDGE

With D, work as foll:

Row 1 (RS) Ch 5, skip 3 sts, *(1 dc, ch 2, 1 dc) in next st, skip 4 sts, ch 3; rep from *, end (1 dc, ch 2; 1 dc) in next st, ch 2, skip 2 sts, dc in last st, turn.

Row 2 Ch 4 (counts as 1 tr), skip first ch-2 space, work 5 tr in next ch-2 space,*skip ch-3 space, 5 tr in next ch-2 sp; rep from *, end 1 tr into 3rd ch of ch-5, turn.

Row 3 Ch 5 (counts as 1 dc and ch 2), skip first 2 tr, (1 dc, ch 2, 1 dc) into next tr, *ch 3, skip 4 tr, (1 dc, ch 2, 1 dc) into next tr; rep from *, end ch 2, 1 dc in top of ch-4, turn. Rep rows 2 and 3 twice more. Rep row 2. Cut D.

Next row (RS) With C, ch 1, work 27 sc evenly across. Cut C. Complete same lace edge on the other end of scarf.

OUTER TRIM

Next row (RS) Working from RS, with B, ch 1 and work sc through back loops to end of row. Do not fasten off, but cont along the long edge of scarf, *work 3 sc in corner then sc evenly along the long edge, 3 sc in corner*, 1 sc through back loops of each st in C; rep between *'s once. Join and fasten off.

Braided fringe

Make 8 for each end.

Cut one length each 32"/81cm long in colors C, E and F for each fringe. Fold in half and attach to scarf as shown. Knot at scarf, braid and knot at 2"/5cm from end. Trim evenly.

artful argyle

Unleash your preppy side with these snazzy mittens worked in an argyle pattern. They'll be a hit on or off campus! Designed by Charlotte Parry, "Artful Argyle" first appeared in the Fall '05 issue of *Family Circle Easy Knitting.*

MITTENS

With MC, work as for striped mittens, page 76. The argyle pattern can be knitted in by centering the 11-stitch chart on the last 17 (21, 25) sts of Rnd 1 on the left mitten and the first 17 (21, 25) sts of Rnd 1 on the right mitten. Work as many 12-rnd reps of the argyle chart as necessary for each size, ending with a row 7. If desired, the design can be embroidered in duplicate stitch after the solid-color mittens have been knitted.

MITTENS SIZED FOR CHILDREN, WOMEN, MEN.

MATERIALS

TLC Essentials by Coats & Clark, 5oz/140g skeins, each approx 326yd/298m (acrylic)

- 1 skein in #2915 cranberry (MC), #2772 rose and #2316 winter white
- Five size 6 (4mm) dp needles, OR SIZE TO OBTAIN GAUGE
- Safety pin or small stitch holder

FINISHED MEASUREMENTS

Length from wrist to fingertips 7 (10,11)"/18 (25.5, 28)cm

Wrist circumference 5¼ (6½, 7½)"/13.5cm (16.5, 19)cm

GAUGE

20 sts and 28 rows to 4"/10cm over St st using size 6 (4mm) needles.

TAKE TIME TO CHECK YOUR GAUGE.

MITTEN CHART

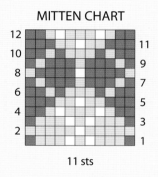

11 sts

Color Key

- ■ Cranberry
- □ Winter white
- ▨ Rose

fast & flirty

Commitment-phobes
can keep their time
to a minimum with
these quick, edgy,
and easy projects.

mesh it up

Sweet and sexy, this mesh coverup will make beaching it a breeze. Long tassels add a decorative edge. Designed by Mari Lynn Patrick, "Mesh It Up" first appeared in the Spring/Summer '05 issue of *Family Circle Easy Knitting.*

MATERIALS

Cotton Tots by Bernat, 4oz/113g balls, each approx 200yd/182m (cotton)

- 3 (4, 4) balls in #90005 white
- Size G/6 (4.5mm) crochet hook OR SIZE TO OBTAIN GAUGE
- Bobbins

FINISHED MEASUREMENTS

Bust 32 (34, 36)"/81 (86, 91.5)cm

Length (excluding fringe) 23½ (24, 24½)"/59.5 (61, 62)cm

GAUGE

3¾ mesh pats and 8 mesh rows to 4"/10cm over mesh pat st using size G/6 (4.5mm) hook.

TAKE TIME TO CHECK YOUR GAUGE.

MESH PATTERN STITCH

Ch a multiple of 4 sts plus 2.

Row 1 (RS) Work 1 sc in 6th ch from hook, *ch 5, skip 3 ch, 1 sc in next ch; rep from * to end, join with sc in beg lp, being careful not to twist sts, and turn.

Row 2 Ch 5 and 1 sc in each ch-5 arch to end, join with sc in first lp and turn.

Rep row 2 for mesh pat. Note that pat is worked back and forth in rows but joined at the end to form a "rnd".

Note To work 2 sc tog: [insert hook in next st and draw up a lp] twice, yo and draw through all 3 lps on hook.

BODY

Beg at lower edge, ch 130 (138, 146). Work in pat on 32 (34, 36) mesh pats until piece measures 6"/15cm from beg. Dec 1 pat at end of next row by eliminating one ch-5 at end of row. Rep dec when piece measures 8"/20.5cm from beg—30 (32, 34) mesh pats. Work even until piece measures 15"/38cm from beg.

SEPARATE FOR ARMHOLES—BACK

Note Place yarn marker at 15th (16th, 17th) ch-5 arch.

Row 1 (RS) Work 3 sl sts into first ch-5 loop, work 13 (14, 15) ch-5 arches, leave marked arch unworked for the underarm and rem 15 (16, 17) arches unworked for front, turn.

Row 2 Ch 1, work 2 sl sts in first ch-5 arch, ch 5 and work 11 (12, 13) ch-5 arches across. Work even on these 11 (12, 13) arches for 7½ (8, 8½)"/19 (20.5, 21.5)cm OR 15 (16, 17) rows.

SHOULDER SHAPING

Next row Work 2 ch-5 arches, turn.

Next row Work 2 ch-5 arches, turn. Fasten off. Skip the center 7 (8, 9) arches and join to last 2 arches and work 2 rows for other shoulder. Fasten off.

FRONT

Row 1 From the WS, skip the first of 15 (16, 17) ch-5 arches for front and join in the sc after the arch, work 13 (14, 15) ch-5 arches, turn.

Row 2 Rep row 2 as on back—11 (12, 13) ch-5 arches. Work even on these arches for 6½ (7, 7½)"/16.5 (18, 19)cm OR 13 (14, 15) rows.

SHOULDER SHAPING

Work across 2 ch-5 arches on one side for 4 rows. Fasten off. Skip the center 7 (8, 9) arches and work the other shoulder in the same way.

FINISHING

Sl st the shoulders tog from WS.

ARMHOLE TRIM

Join with sc in first sc at armhole, *ch 4, sc in next ch-5 loop; rep from *, end by placing last sc in first sc. Fasten off. Rep around rem armhole in same way.

NECK TRIM

Work edge in same way as armhole around the neck.

LOWER TRIM

Row 1 Join with sc in base of any sc, ch 3, *sc in base of next sc, ch 3; rep from * around, join with sl st in first sc. Turn.

Row 2 Ch 1, *sc in next sc, sc in each of next 3 ch (not in the ch-loop); rep from * around, join. Turn.

Row 3 Ch 1, sc in first st, work 2 sc tog, sc to last 3 sc, 2 sc tog, sc in last sc, turn.

Row 4 Ch 1, sc in first st, *ch 4, skip 3 sc, sc in next sc; rep from * to end. Fasten off. For each fringe, cut 3 15"/38cm strands and fringe each sc along lower edge.

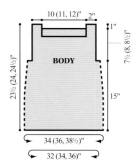

slim waisted

Self-striping yarn moves on from socks in this super cinch of a design from Veronica Manno. All it takes is a couple of D-rings and some seed stitching, and you have a belt to carry you through spring and summer. "Slim Waisted" first appeared in the Fall '04 issue of *Family Circle Easy Knitting*.

MATERIALS

Magic Stripes by Lion Brand Yarn Company, 3½oz/100g balls, each approx 330yd/300m (wool/nylon)

 1 ball in #204 bright spring

 One pair size 4 (3.5mm) needles OR SIZE TO OBTAIN GAUGE

 Two ³/₈"/10mm D-rings from M&J Trimming, art. #10418

GAUGE

 24 sts and 42 rows to 4"/10cm over seed st using size 4 (3.5mm) needles.

 TAKE TIME TO CHECK YOUR GAUGE.

SEED STITCH

Row 1 (RS) *K1, p1; rep from * to end.
Row 2 *P1, k1; rep from * to end.
Rep rows 1 and 2 for seed st.

BELT

Cast on 6 sts. Work in seed st to desired length. Bind off.

FINISHING

Sew two D-rings to one end of belt.

jiffy tube

These sassy separates from Rebecca Rosen are the In Thing. Whether you go striped or solid, you're guaranteed to have the warmest (and cutest) ankles and wrists in town. "Jiffy Tube" first appeared in the Fall '04 issue of *Family Circle Easy Knitting*.

MATERIALS FOR LEG WARMERS

10 Ply by Wool Pak Yarns NZ/Baabajoe's Wool Co., 8oz/250g balls, each approx, 430yd/396m (wool)

   1 ball in #08 plum (A)

   1 ball (or small amount) each in #05 pink (B), #36 red (C), #15 orange (D), #12 forest (E), #27 gold (F)

   One pair size 8 (5mm) needles OR SIZE TO OBTAIN GAUGE

FINISHED MEASUREMENTS

   Width at top 13 (15)"/33 (38)cm

   Length 13 ½"/34.5cm

GAUGE

   16 sts and 20 rows to 4"/10cm over St st using size 8 (5mm) needles. TAKE TIME TO CHECK YOUR GAUGE.

Note

   Instructions are written for a slimmer version (first size) to be worn on their own and a larger version (second size) to fit over pants.

fast & flirty ● ● ● ●

STRIPE PATTERN

Working in St st, work 2 rows B, 2 rows C, 2 rows D, 2 rows E, 2 rows A, 2 rows F. Rep these 12 rows for stripe pat.

SOLID COLOR LEG WARMERS

With A, cast on 52 (60) sts. Work in garter st for 4 rows. Work in St st, dec 1 st each side every 4th row 4 times (every 2nd row 7 times)—44 (46) sts. Work even until piece measures 5"/12.4cm from beg. Cont in St st, inc 1 st each side every 6th row (5) times—56 sts. Work even until piece measures 13 ¼"/33.5cm. Work in garter st for 4 rows. Bind off loosely.

STRIPED LEG WARMERS

With A, cast on 52 (60) sts. Work in garter st for 4 rows. Working decs same as solid version, work 12 rows stripe pat twice. Piece measures appox 5"/12.5cm. Change to B and cont as for solid version.

FINISHING

Sew seam.

MATERIALS FOR WRIST WARMERS

10 Ply by Wool Pak Yarns NZ/Baabajoe's Wool Co., 8oz/250g balls, each approx 430yd/396m (wool)

  1 ball in #05 pink (A)

  1 ball (or small amount) each in #36 red (B), #15 orange (C), #12 forest (D), #08 plum (E) and #27 gold (F)

  One pair size 8 (5mm) needles OR SIZE TO OBTAIN GAUGE

GAUGE

  16 sts and 20 rows to 4"/10cm over St s using size 8 (5mm) needles.

  TAKE TIME TO CHECK YOUR GAUGE.

STRIPE PATTERN

Working in St st, work 2 rows B, 2 rows C, 2 rows D, 2 rows E, 2 rows F.

SOLID COLOR WRIST WARMERS

Right Warmer

With A, cast on 32 sts. Work in garter st for 3 rows. P 1 row. Work in St st until piece measures 1"/2.5cm, end with a WS row.

Thumb opening

Next row (RS) K10, join a 2nd ball of yarn and work to end. Working both sides at once, work even until opening measures 1¼"/3cm, work last RS row with 1 ball to close opening.

Next row (WS) Purl, dec 6 sts evenly across—26 sts.

Next row (RS) K5, *p4, k4; rep from * to last 5 sts, end p5.

Next row (WS) K the knit and p the purl sts. Rep last 2 rows until piece measures 6 from beg, end with a WS row.

Inc. 1 st each side of next row, then every 4th row once more, working inc st at beg of rows as k sts and inc sts at end of rows as p sts—30 sts. Work even until piece measures 8 ½"/21.5cm from beg. Bind off loosely in rib.

LEFT WARMER

Work as for right warmer to thumb opening.

Next row (RS) K22, join a 2nd ball of yarn and work to end. Work as for right warmer to end.

STRIPED WRIST WARMERS

With B, cast on 32 sts. Work in garter st for 3 rows. P 1 row. Work 10 rows of stripe pat. Cont in A, work as for right and left solid color wrist warmers.

FINISHING

Sew seam.

cross your heart

This off-the-shoulder wrap is elegant enough for an old-fashioned dinner party, yet hip enough for a night out dancing. Its center twist brings a touch of surprise. Designed by Linda Cyr, "Cross Your Heart" first appeared in the Spring/Summer '05 issue of *Family Circle Easy Knitting*.

MATERIALS

Katrina by Patons, 3½oz/100g balls, each approx 163yd/150m (rayon/polyester)

- 3 balls each in #10425 dusk
- One pair size 10 (6mm) needles OR SIZE TO OBTAIN GAUGE

FINISHED MEASUREMENTS

Approx 13½" x 46"/34 x 117cm, before edges are joined.

GAUGE

16 sts and 25 rows to 4"/10cm over St st using size 10 (6mm) needles.

TAKE TIME TO CHECK YOUR GAUGE.

WRAP

Cast on 54 sts. Work even in St st until piece measures 46"/117cm from beg. Bind off.

FINISHING

Lightly steam and block. Twisting piece once, sew bound-off edge to cast-on edge to form a tube. To wear, position seam at center back with twist at center front.

bobble socks

Get out your poodle skirt and saddleback shoes! These pompom footwarmers take a trip down memory lane with decorated ribbed cuffs and stockinette-stitch soles. Designed by Charlotte Parry, "Bobble Socks" first appeared in the Holiday '04 issue of *Family Circle Easy Knitting*.

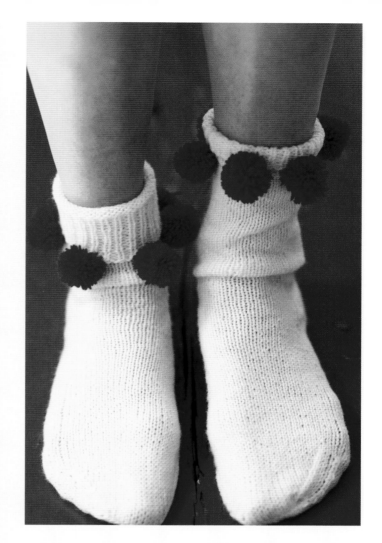

MATERIALS

Fortissima Socka by Schoeller & Stahl/Skacel Collections, 1¾oz/50g balls, each approx 231yd/210m (wool/polyamide)

- 2 balls in #1001 cream (MC)
- 1 ball in #1010 red (CC)
- One pair and one set (4) size 3 (3.25mm) dpn OR SIZE TO OBTAIN GAUGE
- Stitch marker
- Stitch holder

FINISHED MEASUREMENTS

Leg width 7¾"/19.5cm

Foot length 8½"/21.5cm

GAUGE

28 sts and 38 rnds to 4"/10cm over St st using size 3 (3.25mm) needles.

TAKE TIME TO CHECK YOUR GAUGE.

SIZE

Women's socks sized in one size.

CUFF

With MC, loosely cast on 54 sts. Divide sts evenly over 3 needles. Join, taking care not to twist sts on needles. Mark end of rnd and sl marker every rnd. Work in k1, p1 rib for 2"/5cm. Cont in St st until piece measures 7½"/19cm from beg.

HEEL

K13 from first needle, then sl 14 sts from 3rd needle onto other end of first needle—27 heel sts. Sl rem 27 sts to st holder for instep. Work back and forth in St st on 27 sts for 1"/2.5cm, end with a RS row.

Turn heel

Row 1 (WS) P14, p2tog, p1, turn.

Row 2 Sl 1, k2, SKP, k1, turn.

Row 3 Sl 1, p3, p2tog, p1, turn.

Row 4 Sl 1, k4, SKP, k1, turn.

Row 5 Sl 1, p5, p2tog, p1, turn.

Row 6 Sl 1, k6, SKP, k1, turn.

Row 7 Sl 1, p7, p2tog, p1, turn.

Row 8 Sl 1, k8, SKP, k1, turn.

Row 9 Sl 1, p9, p2tog, p1, turn.

Row 10 Sl 1, k10, SKP, k1, turn.

Row 11 Sl 1, p11, p2tog, p1, turn.

Row 12 Sl 1, k12, SKP, k1, turn—15 sts.

Next rnd (RS) With same needle as heel, pick up and k 11 sts along left side (rows) of heel (Needle 1); with another needle, k 27 sts of instep from holder (Needle 2); with another needle, pick up and k 11 sts along right side of heel, then k 7 sts from first (Needle 3). Needle 1 has 19 sts, Needle 2 has 27 sts and Needle 3 has 18 sts—64 total sts. Mark center of heel for end of rnd.

Instep shaping

Rnd 1 Knit.

Rnd 2 Needle 1, k to last 3 sts, k2tog, k1; Needle 2, knit; Needle 3, k1, SKP, k to end. Rep last 2 rnds 4 times more—54 sts.

Work even until foot measures 6¾"/17cm from back of heel or 1"/4.5cm less than desired length from back of heel to end of toe.

Toe shaping

Rnd 1 Needle 1, k to last 3 sts, k2tog, k1; Needle 2, k1, SKP, k to last 3 sts, k2tog, k1; Needle 3, k1, SKP, k to end.

Rnd 2 Knit.

Rep last 2 rnds 6 times more—26 sts. Divide sts evenly onto 2 needles and weave toe sts tog using Kitchener st (see page 112).

FINISHING

Block socks, being careful not to flatten rib. Using CC, make twelve 1"/2.5cm pompoms. Sew 6 evenly spaced around edge of each cuff.

finger lickin' good

Keep hands warm but fingers free. These cropped mittens let you do whatever you need to and still look great—and all it takes is one skein. "Finger Lickin' Good" first appeared in the Winter '01/'02 issue of *Family Circle Easy Knitting.*

MATERIALS

Red Heart® Sport by Coats & Clark 2.5oz/70g balls (acrylic)

1 ball #846 blue

One pair size 6/4mm needle or size to obtain gauge

Stitch markers

GAUGE

20 sts and 28 rows to 4"/10cm over St st using size 6/4mm needles. TAKE TIME TO CHECK YOUR GAUGE.

CUFF

Cast on 40 sts. Row 1 *K2, p2; rep from * to end. Rep row 1 for rib for 2"/5cm.

HAND

Continue in St st (k 1 row on RS, p 1 row on WS) until piece measures 5"/12.5cm from beg, or desired length to thumb, end with a WS row.

TOP SHAPING

Next row (RS) K2, increase 1 st in next st, place marker, k to last 3 sts, place marker, inc 1 st in next st, k2—42 sts. P 1 row. **Next row (RS)** K to 1 st before marker, increase 1 st in next st, slip marker, work to 2nd marker, sl marker, increase 1 st in next st, k to end—44 sts. P 1 row. Rep last 2 rows until there are 52 sts. Bind off 8 sts at beginning of next 2 rows. Work in k2, p2 rib same as cuff for 8 row more. Bind off loosely in rib. Make a second mitt in same way.

FINISHING

Sew side seams.

skirt it!

Small enough to stitch up quick, this crocheted mesh skirt is a cool coverup for a two-piece. Tie a bow on the hip and you're free to run and play! Designed by Jacqueline van Dillen, "Skirt It!" first appeared in the Spring/Summer '05 issue of *Family Circle Easy Knitting*.

MATERIALS

Wildflower D.K. by Plymouth Yarn, 1¾oz/50g balls, each approx 137yd/125m (cotton/acrylic)

- 3 balls in #41 white
- Size E/4 (3.5mm) crochet hook OR SIZE TO OBTAIN GAUGE

FINISHED MEASUREMENTS

Approx 34"/86.5cm around hips

GAUGE

18 hdc to 4"/10cm and 3 hdc rows to 1" using size E/4 (3.5mm) hook.

TAKE TIME TO CHECK YOUR GAUGE.

Note

Skirt is worked from top edge to bottom.

SKIRT

Hip Band

Ch 152.

Row 1 Starting in third ch from hook, work hdc in each ch across—151 sts, counting turning ch as 1 st. Ch 2, turn.

Row 2 Skip first hdc, hdc in each hdc across. Ch 2, turn.

Row 3 Rep row 2.

Skirt

Row 1 Ch 3, skip first 3 hdc, sc in next hdc, *ch 3, skip next 2 hdc, sc in next hdc; rep from * across—50 ch-3 lps. Turn.

Row 2 *Ch 4, sc in next lp; rep from * across.

Rows 3–8 Rep row 2.

Row 9 *[Ch 4, sc in next lp] 3 times, ch 5, sc in next lp; rep from * across, end [ch 4, sc in next lp] twice.

Row 10 *Ch 4, sc in next lp, ch 5, sc in next lp; rep from * across.

Rows 11–18 *Ch 5, sc in next lp; rep from * across.

Row 19 *[Ch 5, sc in next lp] 3 times, ch 6, sc in next lp; rep from * across, end [ch 5, sc in next lp] twice.

Row 20 *Ch 5, sc in next lp, ch 6, sc in next lp; rep from * across.

Rows 21–26 *Ch 6, sc in next lp; rep from * across.

Fasten off after row 26 is completed.

Ties

Row 1 Join yarn with sl st at side edge of hip band, ch 2, work 5 hdc evenly spaced across 3 hdc rows. Ch 2, turn.

Row 2 Skip first hdc, hdc in each hdc across. Ch 2, turn.

Rep row 2 until tie measures approx 18"/46cm. Fasten off. Make another tie on opposite side of hip band in same way.

a-head of the pack

Mari Lynn Patrick's crocheted skullcap is a beachgoer's dream: it lets you feel the salt-air breeze without the chill and looks great with a jeans or a sundress. "A-Head of the Pack" first appeared in the Spring/Summer '03 issue of *Family Circle Easy Knitting.*

MATERIALS
Grace by Patons®, 1¾oz/50g balls, each approx 136yd/125m (cotton)

    1 ball in #60005 white

    One each sizes E/4/ (3.5mm) and G/6 (4.5mm) crochet hooks

    OR SIZE TO OBTAIN GAUGE

FINISHED MEASUREMENTS
    Head circumference 20"/51cm

    Depth 6½"/16.5cm

GAUGE
    3 cluster pats and 4 rnds to 4"/10cm using size G/6 (4.5mm) hook.

    TAKE TIME TO CHECK YOUR GAUGE.

CAP
Beg at crown, with size G/6 (4.5mm) crochet hook, ch 4, join with sl st to first ch to form ring.

Rnd 1 Work 9 sc into ring, join with sl st to first sc.

Rnd 2 Ch 1, work 2 sc in each sc around, join with sl st to first sc—18 sc.

Rnd 3 Ch 3, * in next sc work 1 dc, ch 2 and 1 dc (for V-st), skip 2 sc, ch 3; rep from * 5 times more, end by joining with sl st in top of first ch-3—6 V-sts.

Rnd 4 Ch 4, *5tr in ch 2-sp (for cluster), skip ch-3sp, ch 2; rep from * 5 times more, end with sl st in top of ch-4—6 clusters.

Rnd 5 Ch 6, *skip 2 tr, in next tr work 1 dc, ch 2 and 1 dc (for V-st), ch 3, in next ch 2-sp work V-st, ch 3; rep from * end skip 2tr, in next tr work V-st, ch 3, dc in same sp with ch-6, ch 2, sl st in 3rd ch of ch-6—12 V-sts.

Rnd 6 Ch 6, *5 tr in next V-st, ch 3; rep from * 11 times more, end join with sl st in 4th ch of ch-6—12 clusters.

Rnd 7 Ch 6, *[in center tr of next 5-tr cluster work 1 V-st, ch 3] 3 times, V-st in next ch-3 sp, ch 3; rep from * twice more, then [in center tr of next 5-tr cluster work V-st, ch 3] 3 times, sl st in 3rd ch of ch-6—15 V-sts.

Rnd 8 Ch 6, *5 tr in next V-st, ch 2; rep from * 14 times more, end join with sl st in 4th ch of ch 6—15 clusters.

Rnd 9 Ch 6, * in center of next 5-tr cluster work 1 V-st, ch 3; rep from * 14 times more, end with sl st in 3rd ch of ch-6—15 V-sts.

Rnds 10 and 12 Rep rnd 8.

Rnd 11 Rep rnd 9.

Rnd 13 Ch 1, * work 1 sc in ch-2 sp, 1 sc in each of 5 tr; rep from *, end 1 sc in last ch-2 sp, join with sl to first sc—91 sc.

Rnd 14 Ch 3, skip next sc, *1 dc in next 2 sc, ch 1, skip 1 sc; rep from *, end sl st to 2nd ch of ch-3.

Change to size E/4 (3.5mm) hook and turn to WS to work last 2 rnds from WS.

Rnd 15 (WS) Ch 1, work 1 sc in each dc and in each ch-1 around.

Rnd 16 (WS) Ch 3, skip first sc, * work 1 dc and 1 hdc in next sc, sl st in next sc; rep from * around. Fasten off.

tie one on

Move over, boys, this one's for the girls! Mari Lynn Patrick's tie is stitched diagonally for maximum texture and looks polished on anyone—male or female. "Tie One On" first appeared in the Fall '04 issue of *Family Circle Easy Knitting*.

MATERIALS

Grace by Patons®, 1¾oz/50g balls, each approx 136yd/125m (cotton)

- 2 balls in #60108 dk blue
- One pair size 2 (2.75mm) needles OR SIZE TO OBTAIN GAUGE

FINISHED MEASUREMENTS

59"/150cm long and 3½"/9cm wide (at widest point)

GAUGE

28 sts and 44 rows to 4"/10cm over diagonal pat st using size 2 (2.75mm) needles.

TAKE TIME TO CHECK YOUR GAUGE.

DIAGONAL PATTERN STITCH

(over a multiple of 4 sts plus 4 selvage sts).

Row 1 (WS) K2, *k2, p2; rep from *, end k2.

Row 2 (RS) K2, *k1, p2, k1; rep from *, end k2.

Row 3 K2, *p2, k2; rep from *, end k2.

Row 4 K2, *p1, k2, p1; rep from *, end k2. Rep rows 1-4 for diagonal pat st.

TIE

Beg at large-pointed end, cast on 3 sts.

Row 1 (RS) K3.

Row 2 K1, M1, k2.

Row 3 K4

Row 4 K2, M1, k2.

Row 5 K2, M1, k3.

Row 6 K2, M1, p2, k2—7 sts.

Row 7 K2, M1, k2, p1, k2—8 sts.

Row 8 K2, M1, k2, p2, k2.

Row 9 K2, M1, k1, p2, k2, p1, k2—11 sts.

Rows 11–23 Cont to work in this way, foll chart and working first 2 sts and last 2 sts in garter st and M1 after these 2 sts at beg of every row 13 times more—24 sts. Place yarn markers ech end of last row. Then work as established in diagonal pat st (rep rows 24-27 of chart) until tie measures 4"/10cm from yarn markers.

Dec row (RS) K2, SKP, work diagonal pat st to last 4 sts, k2tog, k2—22 sts. Rep dec row every 4"/10cm 3 times more, every 3"/7.5cm 3 times more—10 sts. Work even until tie measures 56"/142cm from yarn markers.

Short point shaping

Next row (RS) Work dec row. Work 1 row even. Rep last 2 rows twice more—4sts.

Last row k1, SKP, k1. Bind off remaining 3 sts.

FINISHING

Lay tie flat, stretching slightly and block to measurements.

shrug it on

Keep spring chills at bay with this light and easy ribbed shawlette. Fringed edges keep the theme lighthearted! "Shrug It on" was designed by Jill Schoenfuss for the Spring/Summer '05 issue of *Family Circle Easy Knitting.*

MATERIALS

Aerie by Moda Dea/Coats & Clark, 1¾oz/50g balls, each approx 71yd/65m (nylon)

　3 (4, 4, 4) balls in #9113 in ecru (MC)

Tiara by Moda Dea/Coats & Clark, 1¾oz/50g balls, each approx 46yd/42m (polyester)

　2 (3, 3, 3) balls in #4913 in sand lot (CC)

　One pair size 10 (6mm) needles, OR SIZE TO OBTAIN GAUGE

　Stitch markers

FINISHED MEASUREMENTS

　Approx 9 (9, 10, 10)" x 32 (34, 36, 38)"/23 (23, 25.5, 25.5)cm x 81.5 (86.5, 91.5, 96.5)cm

NOTE

　A knitted length of 32"/81.5cm is sufficient to fit a shoulder measurement of 38"/96.5cm. For best sizing, fit as you knit.

GAUGE

　13 sts and 24 rows over 4"/10cm in pat st using size 10 (6mm) needles.

　TAKE TIME TO CHECK YOUR GAUGE.

PATTERN STITCH

Row 1 With MC, k24 (24, 26, 26), pick up CC and with MC and CC held tog k6 (6, 7, 7).

Row 2 With MC and CC held tog, p6 (6, 7, 7), drop CC, with MC only p18 (18, 19, 19), k6 (6, 7, 7).

Row 3 Rep row 1.

Row 4 With MC and CC held tog, k6 (6, 7, 7), drop CC, with MC only k24 (24, 26, 26).

Row 5 With MC, k6 (6, 7, 7), p18 (19), pick up CC and with MC and CC held tog, k6 (6, 7, 7).

Row 6 Rep row 4.

Rep rows 1-6 for pat st.

SHAWLETTE

With MC, cast on 30 (30, 33, 33) sts. Work in pat st. If desired, place markers after first 6 (7) sts and before last 6 (7) sts. Cont in pat st until piece measures 32 (34, 36, 38)"/81.5 (86.5, 91.5, 96.5)cm, or desired length to fit around shoulders, end with a pat row 6.

Note Keep in mind that this is a stretchy fabric. Bind off all sts.

FINISHING

Weave in any ends. Fold piece in half and sew cast-on and bound-off edges tog for back seam.

basics

SIZING

Since clothing measurements have changed in recent decades, it is very important to measure yourself carefully to determine which size is best for you.

YARN SELECTION

For an exact reproduction of the projects photographed, use the yarn listed in the "Materials" section of the pattern. We've chosen yarns that are readily available in the U.S. and Canada at the time of printing. The Resources guide on page 143 provides addresses of yarn distributors. Contact them for the name of a retailer in your area.

YARN SUBSTITUTION

If you want to work with a different yarn, by all means do so. Perhaps you view small-scale projects as a chance to incorporate leftovers from your stash, or the yarn specified may not be available in your area. You'll need to knit to the given gauge to obtain the knitted measurements with a substitute yarn (see "Gauge" at right). Be sure to consider how the fiber content of the substitute yarn will affect the comfort and the ease of care of your projects.

After you've successfully gauge-swatched a substitute yarn, you'll need to figure out how much of the new yarn the project requires. First, find the total length of the original yarn in the pattern (multiply number of balls by yards/meters per ball). Divide this figure by the new yards/meters per ball (listed on the ball band). Round up to the next whole number. The result is the number of balls required.

LACE

Lace knitting provides a feminine touch. Knitted lace is formed with "yarn overs," which create an eyelet hole in combination with decreases that create directional effects. To make a yarn over (yo), merely pass the yarn over the right-hand needle to form a new loop. Decreases are worked as k2tog, ssk, or SKP depending on the desired slant and are spelled out specifically with each instruction. On the row or round that follows the lace or eyelet detail, each yarn over is treated as one stitch. If you're new to lace knitting, it's a good idea to count the stitches at the end of each row or round. Making a gauge swatch in the stitch pattern enables you to practice the lace pattern. Instead of binding off the swatch, place the final row on a holder, as the bind off tends to pull in the stitches and distort the gauge.

COLORWORK KNITTING

Two main types of colorwork are explored in this book.

Intarsia

Intarsia is accomplished with separate bobbins of individual colors. This method is ideal for large blocks of color or for motifs that aren't repeated close together. When changing colors, always pick up the new shade and wrap it around the old one.

Stranding

When motifs are closely placed, colorwork is accomplished by stranding along two or more colors per row, creating "floats" on the wrong side of the fabric. This technique is sometimes called Fair Isle knitting after the traditional Fair Isle patterns that are composed of small motifs with frequent color changes.

To keep an even tension and prevent holes pick up yarns alternately over and under one another across or around. While knitting, stretch the stitches on the needle slightly wider than the length of the float at the back to keep work from puckering.

When changing colors at the beginning of rows or rounds, carry yarn along for a few rows only, or cut yarn and rejoin when needed. It is important to keep the "floats" small and neat so they don't catch when pulling on the piece.

GAUGE

It is still important to knit a gauge swatch to assure a perfect fit in a garment. If the gauge is incorrect, a colorwork pattern may become distorted. The type of needles used—straight, circular, wood or metal—will influence gauge, so knit your swatch with the needles you plan to use for the project. Measure gauge as illustrated here. (Launder and block your gauge swatch before taking measurements). Try different needle sizes until your sample measures the required number of stitches and rows. To get fewer stitches to the inch/cm, use larger needles; to get more stitches to the inch/cm, use smaller needles. It's a good idea to keep your gauge swatch to test any embroidery or embellishment, as well as for blocking and cleaning methods.

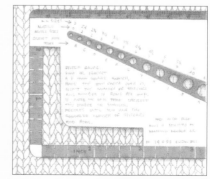

BASIC STITCHES

GARTER STITCH
Knit every row. Circular knitting: knit one round, then purl one round.

STOCKINETTE STITCH
Knit right-side rows and purl wrong-side rows. Circular knitting: knit all rounds. (UK: stocking stitch)

REVERSE STOCKINETTE STITCH
Purl right-side rows and knit wrong-side rows. Circular knitting: purl all rounds. (UK: reverse stocking stitch)

STOCKINETTE STITCH I-CORD
Using two double-pointed needles, cast on 3, 4, 5 or 6 stitches.
Row 1 K3, 4, 5 or 6, do not turn, slide sts to other end of needle. Rep row 1 for desired length.

BLOCKING
Blocking is an all-important finishing step in the knitting process. It is the best way to shape pattern pieces and smooth knitted edges in preparation for sewing together. Most garments retain their shape if the blocking stages in the instructions are followed carefully. Choose a blocking method according to the yarn care label and when in doubt, test-block your gauge swatch.

WET BLOCK METHOD
Using rust-proof pins, pin pieces to measurements on a flat surface and lightly dampen using a spray bottle. Allow to dry before removing pins.

STEAM BLOCK METHOD
With WS facing, pin pieces. Steam lightly, holding the iron 2"/5cm above the knitting. Do not press or it will flatten stitches.

FINISHING
The pieces in this book use a variety of finishing techniques. Directions for making a simple fringe is on the bottom right of this page. Also refer to the illustrations such as "To Begin Seaming" and "Invisible Seaming: Stockinette St" provided for other useful techniques.

CARE
Refer to the yarn label for the recommended cleaning method. Many of the projects in the book can be either washed by hand, or in the machine on a gentle or wool cycle, in lukewarm water with a mild detergent. Do not agitate, or soak for more than 10 minutes. Rinse gently with tepid water, then fold in a towel and gently press the water out. Lay flat to dry away from excess heat and light. Check the yarn band for any specific care instructions such as dry cleaning or tumble drying.

SKILL LEVELS

beginner
Ideal first project.

easy ● ● ● ●
Basic stitches, minimal shaping, simple finishing.

intermediate ● ● ● ●
For knitters with some experience. More intricate stitches, shaping, and finishing.

experienced ● ● ● ●
For knitters able to work patterns with complicated shaping and finishing.

KNITTING NEEDLES		CROCHET HOOKS	
US	METRIC	US	METRIC
0	2mm	B/1	2.25mm
1	2.25mm	C/2	2.75mm
2	2.75mm		
3	3.25mm	D/3	3.25mm
4	3.5mm	E/4	3.5mm
5	3.75mm	F/5	3.75mm
6	4mm		
7	4.5mm	G/6	4mm
8	5mm	7	4.5mm
9	5.5mm	H/8	5mm
10	6mm	I/9	5.5mm
10½	6.5mm		
11	8mm	J/10	6mm
13	9mm	K/10½	6.5mm
15	10mm	L/11	8mm
17	12.75mm		
19	15mm	M/13	9mm
35	19mm	N/15	10mm

SIMPLE FRINGE

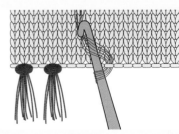

Cut yarn twice desired length plus extra for knotting. On wrong side, insert hook from front to back through piece and over folded yarn. Pull yarn through. Draw ends through and tighten. Trim yarn.

basics

TO BEGIN SEAMING

If you have left a long tail from your cast-on row, you can use this strand to begin sewing. To make a neat join at the lower edge with no gap, use the technique shown here. Thread the strand into a yarn needle. With the right sides of both pieces facing you, insert the yarn needle from back to front into the corner stitch of the piece without the tail. Making a figure eight with the yarn, insert the needle from back to front into the stitch with the cast-on tail. Tighten to close the gap.

INVISIBLE SEAMING: STOCKINETTE ST

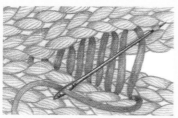

To make an invisible side seam in a garment worked in stockinette stitch, insert the tapestry needle under the horizontal bar between the first and second stitches. Insert the needle into the corresponding bar on the other piece. Pull the yarn gently until the sides meet. Continue alternating from side to side.

TASSELS

Cut a piece of cardboard to the desired length of the tassel. Wrap yarn around the cardboard. Knot a piece of yarn tightly around one end, cut as shown, and remove the cardboard. Wrap and tie yarn around the tassel about 1"/2.5cm down from the top to secure the fringe.

CROCHET STITCHES

CHAIN

1 Pass the yarn over the hook and catch it with the hook.

2 Draw the yarn through the loop on the hook.

3 Repeat steps 1 and 2 to make a chain.

SINGLE CROCHET

1 Insert the hook through top two loops of a stitch. Pass the yarn over the hook and draw up a loop—two loops on hook.

2 Pass the yarn over the hook and draw through both loops on hook.

3 Continue in the same way, inserting the hook into each stitch.

HALF-DOUBLE CROCHET

1 Pass the yarn over the hook. Insert the hook through the top two loops of a stitch.

2 Pass the yarn over the hook and draw up a loop—three loops on hook. Pass the yarn over the hook.

3 Draw through all three loops on hook.

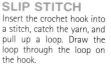

DOUBLE CROCHET

1 Pass the yarn over the hook. Insert the hook through the top two loops of a stitch.

2 Pass the yarn over the hook and draw up a loop—three loops on hook.

3 Pass the yarn over the hook and draw it through the first two loops on the hook, pass the yarn over the hook and draw through the remaining two loops. Continue in the same way, inserting the hook into each stitch.

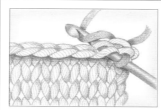

SLIP STITCH

Insert the crochet hook into a stitch, catch the yarn, and pull up a loop. Draw the loop through the loop on the hook.

MULTIPLE YARN OVERS (TWO OR MORE)

Wrap the yarn around the needle, as when working a single yarn over, then continue wrapping the yarn around the needle as many times as indicated. The illustration on the left shows two wraps. Work the next stitch of the left-hand needle. On the following row, work stitches into the extra yarn overs as described in the pattern. The illustration on the right depicts a finished yarn over on the purl side after two stitches have been worked into the double yarn over.

POMPOMS

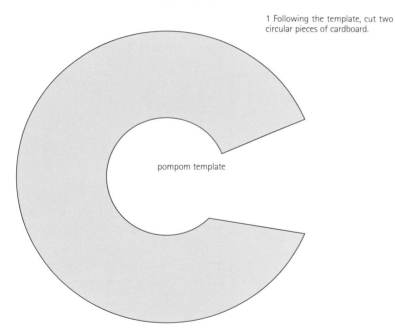

pompom template

1 Following the template, cut two circular pieces of cardboard.

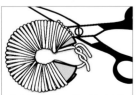

2 Place tie strand between the circles. Wrap yarn around circles. Cut between circles.

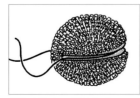

3 Knot tie strand tightly. Remove cardboard.

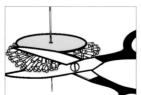

4 Place pompom between two smaller cardboard circles held together with a long needle and trim edges.

DOUBLE-POINTED NEEDLES

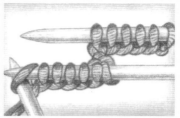

1 Cast on the required number of stitches on the first needle, plus one extra. Slip this extra stitch to the next needle as shown. Continue in this way, casting on the required number of stitches on the last needle.

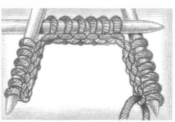

2 Arrange the needles as shown, with the cast-on edge facing the center of the triangle (or square).

3 Place a stitch marker after the last cast-on stitch. With the free needle, knit the first cast-on stitch, pulling the yarn tightly. Continue knitting in rounds, slipping the marker before beginning each round.

knit/crochet terms and abbreviations

approx approximately

beg begin(ning)

bind off Used to finish an edge and keep stitches from unraveling. Lift the first stitch over the second, the second over the third, etc. (UK: cast off)

cast on A foundation row of stitches placed on the needle in order to begin knitting.

CC contrast color

ch chain(s)

cm centimeter(s)

cont continu(e)(ing)

dc double crochet (UK: tr–treble)

dec decrease(ing)–Reduce the stitches in a row (knit 2 together).

dpn double-pointed needle(s)

dtr double treble (UK: trtr–triple treble)

foll follow(s)(ing)

g gram(s)

garter stitch Knit every row. Circular knitting: knit one round, then purl one round.

grp(s) group(s)

hdc half double crochet (UK: htr–half treble)

inc increase(ing)–Add stitches in a row (knit into the front and back of a stitch).

k knit

k2tog knit 2 stitches together

LH left-hand

lp(s) loop(s)

m meter(s)

M1 make one stitch–With the needle tip, lift the strand between last stitch worked and next stitch on the left-hand needle and knit into the back of it. One stitch has been added.

MC main color

mm millimeter(s)

no stitch On some charts, "no stitch" is indicated with shaded spaces where stitches have been decreased or not yet made. In such cases, work the stitches of the chart, skipping over the "no stitch" spaces.

oz ounce(s)

p purl

p2tog purl 2 stitches together

pat(s) pattern

pick up and knit (purl) Knit (or purl) into the loops along an edge.

pm place markers–Place or attach a loop of contrast yarn or purchased stitch marker as indicated.

psso pass slip stitch(es) over

rem remain(s)(ing)

rep repeat

rev St st reverse stockinette stitch–Purl right-side rows, knit wrong-side rows. Circular knitting: purl all rounds. (UK: reverse stocking stitch)

rnd(s) round(s)

RH right-hand

RS right side(s)

sc single crochet (UK: dc–double crochet)

sk skip

SKP Slip 1, knit 1, pass slip stitch over knit 1.

SK2P Slip 1, knit 2 together, pass slip stitch over the knit 2 together.

sl slip–An unworked stitch made by passing a stitch from the left-hand to the right-hand needle as if to purl.

sl st slip stitch (UK: sc–single crochet)

sp(s) space(s)

ssk slip, slip, knit–Slip next 2 stitches knitwise, one at a time, to right-hand needle. Insert tip of left-hand needle into fronts of these stitches from left to right. Knit them together. One stitch has been decreased.

sssk Slip next 3 sts knitwise, one at a time, to right-hand needle. Insert tip of left-hand needle into fronts of these stitches from left to right. Knit them together. Two stitches have been decreased.

st(s) stitch(es)

St st stockinette stitch–Knit right-side rows, purl wrong-side rows. Circular knitting: knit all rounds. (UK: stocking stitch)

tbl through back of loop

t-ch turning chain

tog together

tr treble (UK: dtr–double treble)

trtr triple treble (UK: qtr–quadruple treble)

WS wrong side(s)

wyib with yarn in back

wyif with yarn in front

work even Continue in pattern without increasing or decreasing. (UK: work straight)

yd yard(s)

yo yarn over–Make a new stitch by wrapping the yarn over the right-hand needle. (UK: yfwd, yon, yrn)

* = Repeat directions following * as many times as indicated.

[ ] = Repeat directions inside brackets as many times as indicated.

resources

Write to US resources for mail-order availability of yarns not listed.

US RESOURCES

Write to the yarn companies listed below for purchasing and mail-order information.

Adrienne Vittadini
distributed by
JCA, INC.

Artful Yarns
distributed by
JCA, INC.

Bernat
P. O. Box 40
Listowel, ON N4W 3H3

Berrocco, inc.
P. O. Box 367
Uxbridge, MA 01569

Blue Sky Alpacas
P. O. Box 387
St. Francis, MN 55070

Brown Sheep Co.
100662 County Road 16
Mitchell, NE 69357

Caron International
1481 W. 2ND STREET
Washington, NC 27889

Cascade Yarns, Inc.
1224 Andover Parke
Tukwila, WA 98188-3905

Classic Elite Yarns
300A Jackson Street
Lowell, MA 01852

Cleckheaton
distributed by
Plymouth Yarn

Coats & Clark
Attn: Consumer Service
P. O. Box 12229
Greenville, SC 29612-0229

Colinette
distributed by
Unique Kolours

Di Vé
distributed by
Cascade Yarns, Inc.

GGH
distributed by
Muench Yarns

JCA, Inc.
35 Scales Lane
Townsend, MA 01469

J & P Coats
distributed by
Coats & Clark

Judi & Co.
18 Gallatin Drive
Dix Hills, NY 11746

Lane Borgasesia
distributed by
Trendsetter Yarns

Lion Brand Yarn Co.
34 West 15th Street
New York, NY 10011

Lorna's Laces Yarns
4229 N. Honore St.
Chicago, IL 60613

Moda Dea
distributed by
Coats & Clark

Muench Yarns
1323 Scott Street
Petaluma, CA 94954

Naturally
distributed by
S. R. Kertzer, Ltd.

Needful Yarns, Inc.
4476 Chesswood Drive Suite Unit 10—11
Toronto, ON M3J 2B9
Canada

Patons
P. O. Box 40
Listowel, ON N4W 3H3

Plymouth Yarn
P. O Box 28
Bristol, PA 19007

Reynolds
distributed by
JCA, Inc.

S. Charles Collezione
distributed by
Tahki•Stacy Charles, Inc.

Schoeller & Stahl
distributed by
Skacel Collection

Schelana
distributed by
Skacel Collection

Skacel Collection
P. O. Box 88110
Seattle, WA 98138-2110

S. R. Kertzer, Ltd.
105A Winges Road
Woodbridge, ON L4L 6C2

Tahki•Stacy Charles, Inc.
70-30 80th Street
Bldg. 36
Ridgewood, NY 11385

Trendsetter Yarns
16745 Saticoy Street, #101
Van Nuys, CA 91406

Unique Kolours
28 North Bacton Hill Road
Malvern, PA 19355

CANADIAN RESOURCES

Write to US resources for mail-order availability of yarns not listed.

Berroco, Inc.
distributed by
S. R. Kertzer, Ltd.

Coats & Clark Canada
6060 Burnside Court
Mississauga, ON L5T 2T5

Diamond Yarn
9697 St. Laurent
Montreal, PQ H3L 2N1
and
155 Martin Ross, Unit #3
Toronto, ON M3J 2L9

Domcord Belding
660 Denison St.
Markham, ON L3R 1C1

Les Fils Muench, Canada
5640 Rue Valcourt
Brossard, PQ J4W 1C5

Lion Brand Yarn
distributed by
Domcord Belding

Muench Yarns, Inc.
distributed by
Les Fils Muench, Canada

Naturally
distributed by
S. R. Kertzer, Ltd.

Needful Yarns, Inc.
4476 Chesswood Drive, Suite Unit 10—11
Tornoto, ON M3J 2B9

Patons
P. O. Box 40
Listowel, ON N4W 3H

Rowan
distributed by
Diamond Yarn

S. R. Kertzer, Ltd.
105A Winges Rd.
Woodbridge, ON L4L 6C2

photo credits

Paul Amato
(pp. 8, 9, 14, 22, 26, 28,
29, 34, 35, 37, 42, 44, 54, 58,
63, 64, 71, 72, 76, 89, 90, 98, 112)

Colette
(pp. 83, 84, 94)

Jack Deutsch
(pp. 16, 30, 129)

Dan Howell
(pp. 75, 78, 93, 120, 121, 122)

Roberto Ligresti
(pp. 115, 119, 134)

Francis Milon
(pp. 52, 57)

Nick Norwood
(pp. 6, 12, 24, 32, 46, 114, 116, 130, 132)

Marco Zambelli
(pp. 7, 10, 11, 18, 20, 38, 40, 41, 43, 49, 51,
60, 67, 69, 70, 80, 81, 86, 87, 96,
97, 100, 101, 102, 104, 105, 108,
109, 124, 126, 127, 136)